THE CLASSROOM GUIDE TO JAZZ IMPROVISATION

THE CLASSROOM GUIDE TO JAZZ IMPROVISATION

John McNeil
Ryan Nielsen

OXFORD
UNIVERSITY PRESS

Oxford University Press is a department of the University of Oxford. It furthers
the University's objective of excellence in research, scholarship, and education
by publishing worldwide. Oxford is a registered trade mark of Oxford University
Press in the UK and certain other countries.

Published in the United States of America by Oxford University Press
198 Madison Avenue, New York, NY 10016, United States of America.

© Oxford University Press 2024

All rights reserved. No part of this publication may be reproduced, stored in
a retrieval system, or transmitted, in any form or by any means, without the
prior permission in writing of Oxford University Press, or as expressly permitted
by law, by license, or under terms agreed with the appropriate reproduction
rights organization. Inquiries concerning reproduction outside the scope of the
above should be sent to the Rights Department, Oxford University Press, at the
address above.

You must not circulate this work in any other form
and you must impose this same condition on any acquirer.

Library of Congress Cataloging-in-Publication Data
Names: McNeil, John, 1948- author. | Nielsen, Ryan, author.
Title: The classroom guide to jazz improvisation / John McNeil, Ryan Nielsen.
Description: [1.] | New York : Oxford University Press, 2024. | Includes index.
Identifiers: LCCN 2023040406 (print) | LCCN 2023040407 (ebook) |
ISBN 9780197614655 (paperback) | ISBN 9780197614648 (hardback) |
ISBN 9780197614679 (epub)
Subjects: LCSH: Improvisation (Music) | Jazz—Instruction and study.
Classification: LCC MT68 .M4 2024 (print) | LCC MT68 (ebook) |
DDC 781.65/136—dc23
LC record available at https://lccn.loc.gov/2023040406
LC ebook record available at https://lccn.loc.gov/2023040407

DOI: 10.1093/oso/9780197614648.001.0001

Paperback printed by Marquis Book Printing, Canada
Hardback printed by Bridgeport National Bindery, Inc., United States of America

Dedication

We dedicate this book to Clark Terry, a jazz musician of monumental proportions. The basic principles found here come from Clark's observations about teaching jazz in a more successful and genuine way.

Clark was a technical wizard and a melodicist at the same time—an original, creative trumpet voice if ever there was one. He could play blazing tempos, scream a double G at will, and then break your heart with three notes. Miles Davis, another original guy, said C.T. was a big influence, and you can definitely hear it.

Clark Terry loved and believed in the America that should be and took it upon himself to help change society.

Though rarely credited for it, Clark was singularly responsible for breaking the color line in the New York studio scene. Like Jackie Robinson, he was highly skilled in all aspects of his profession, including how he dealt with other people. For two lonely, high-pressure years, he was the only one in the fire while everyone around waited for him to make a mistake. (Spoiler alert: he never did.) Great black musicians such as Snooky Young, the long-time lead player with Count Basie, would say outright that Clark made it possible for them to make a living in the studios after being shut out for decades.

Because he was perceptive and clever and had a magnetic personality, Clark Terry was always in demand as a jazz adjudicator and clinician. He had an insightful mind and could always see or hear what a young player needed to work on, and how to work on it.

Twenty or so years before this book was printed Clark began expressing his dissatisfaction with the results of jazz education as it was structured. It seemed to him that jazz students, even the younger ones, were not improvising at a high enough level. He felt that what was lacking was their ability to improvise lines that actually sounded like the chord changes. To Clark it seemed like they were just playing notes willy-nilly and the lines that resulted wandered around with no inherent feeling of tonality or chord quality. He never blamed the students; he blamed those that didn't teach them to hear the harmonic implications of what they were playing.

Inspired by who he is and was—personally, pedagogically, and musically—we dedicate this book to him. We sincerely hope that, on some level, it's a continuation of the seeds he cultivated throughout his life.

—*John McNeil and Ryan Nielsen*

A personal note

Always ready to help young players, Clark Terry was the first guy to encourage me, and he told me to plan on moving to New York. Basically, he got me in a headlock and dragged me there.

He started sending me postcards and the occasional letter, and then there were the phone calls. The last one was at 3:00 a.m. I had only been asleep for about 20 minutes because I had had a gig that night. Predictably, I grabbed the phone, hit myself in the face with it and then managed a weak, "Uuh, hel-hello, hello."

It was Clark calling from France. His first question was why I didn't have a 212 area code yet (at that time, 212 was pretty much all of New York City). Somehow, he got me to commit to a definite date when I would be there.

After we hung up, I sat there in the dark and let it sink in. My life as I knew it was going to be over in three months. As it turned out, it was exactly what I had needed. Surprise.

—*John McNeil, New York City, 2022*

CONTENTS

PREFACE XI

ACKNOWLEDGMENTS XIII

CHAPTER 1 GETTING STARTED 1
Everyone Can Improvise 1
Training the Subconscious to Make Choices 1
Beyond Rote Memory 2
How to Use This Book 2
    Lesson Plans for Chapters 2–10, 12–13, 15–16 3
    Appendices 4
    Harmonic Concepts 4
Tips for Getting Started 4
    Incorporating Rhythm 5
Reconsidering Beginning with the Blues 5

CHAPTER 2 BASIC CONCEPTS: THE ROOT TRIAD AND JAZZ RHYTHMS 7
Chord Versus Scale 7
Reading Jazz Chord Symbols 7
    Root 7
    Quality 8
    Minor 8
    Major 8
    Extensions (Notes Higher than the 5th) 8
    Exceptions to the three-part Chord Symbol 9
Lesson Plan 1: Improvising on the Root Triad 9
    How to Create a Background 12
    Rhythm Section 12
Lesson Plan 2: Adding Rhythm 12
Teacher's Notes 16
    Why Start with the Triad? 16
    Choosing Chords to Begin With 16
    Adjusting Range 16
    Designing Rhythm 16
    Rhythm Section 17
        General Tips 17
        Piano: Basic Voicings 18

Guitar: Basic Voicings   20
Bass: Walking Bass Lines with Triad Pitches   21
Drums: Basic Ride Cymbal Technique, Hi-Hat Usage, and Kicks   22

CHAPTER 3   ADDING THE 2ND (1-2-3-5)   25

Lesson Plan 3: Adding the 2nd Degree   25

Lesson Plan 4: Building Longer 8th-Note Lines   27

Teacher's Notes   30
- Other Possibilities on 1-2-3-5   30
- Moving from Chord to Chord   31
- The Metronome in Rehearsal   32
- Tunes to Begin With   32
- More Advanced Rhythms (3/4 + 2/4)   32
- Rhythm Section   34
  - Bass   34

CHAPTER 4   APPROACHING CHORD TONES FROM BELOW   35

Lesson Plan 5: Approach Tones (Half-Step Below)   35

Teacher's Notes   37
- Upbeats and Anticipation   37
- Different Chord Qualities (Major)   38
- Rhythm Section   38
  - Drums: Lightly Kicking Upbeats   38
  - Piano/Guitar: Approaching 3, 7 | 5, 9 Voicings from Below   38

CHAPTER 5   APPROACHING CHORD TONES FROM ABOVE   41

Lesson Plan 6: Approaching Chord Tones from a Scale Step Above   41

Lesson Plan 7: 8th-Note Lines with Approach Tones   43

Teacher's Notes   46
- Rhythm Section   46
  - Bass: Adding Approach Tones to Bass Lines   46
  - Piano   46

CHAPTER 6   APPROACHING CHORD TONES BY TWO NOTES   47

Lesson Plan 8: Two-Note Approach Tones (Above/Below)   47

Lesson Plan 9: Approaching Chord Tones from Two Notes Above or Two Notes Below   49

CHAPTER 7   APPROACHING CHORD TONES BY THREE OR MORE NOTES   53

Lesson Plan 10: Approaching with Three Notes (Part 1)   53

Lesson Plan 11: Approaching with Three Notes (Part 2)   55

Lesson Plan 12: Approaching the 7th   58

Teacher's Notes   60
- Approaching with Four or Five Notes   60
- Simplifying Three-Note Approaches for Less Experienced Students   61

CHAPTER 8   IMPROVISING ON THE ENTIRE CHORD/SCALE (PART 1)   63

Lesson Plan 13: Diatonic Thirds   63

Teacher's Notes   66

Singing Tetrachords 66
Adding Syncopation to Diatonic Thirds 67
More Advanced Use of Thirds 68
Descending Lines 68
Rhythm Section 68
- Bass: Using Diatonic Thirds in Bass Lines 68
- Piano: Using Diatonic Thirds in Comping 69

CHAPTER 9 IMPROVISING ON THE ENTIRE CHORD/SCALE (PART 2): LONGER LINES AND HARMONIC CHANGES 71

Lesson Plan 14: Creating Longer Lines with 3rds 71

Lesson Plan 15: Moving from One Chord/Scale to Another 72

CHAPTER 10 GENERAL SCALE SKILLS: TRIADS, 7TH CHORDS, AND OTHER INTERVALS 77

Lesson Plan 16: Triads and Other Structures 77

Lesson Plan 17: Mixing It Up 79

Teacher's Notes 80
- Organizing Other Structures in the Chord/Scale (7th-Chords, Intervals) 80
- Combining Lessons 81

CHAPTER 11 UNDERSTANDING CHORD SYMBOLS AND RESPELLING CHORDS 83

First, Chord Symbols 83

What Is Respelling? 83

How to Respell 84

Examples of Respelling 85

Extra Credit: Parallel Structures 87

Teacher's Notes 88
- Respelling the Dominant 88
- Respelling the Altered Dominant 88
- Respelling the Half-Diminished Chord 89
- Respelling Lydian 89
- Rhythm Section 89
  - Bass: Only Respell When Soloing 89
  - Piano/Guitar: Voicing the Altered Dominant, When to Respell 90

CHAPTER 12 THE II–7 | V7 | IΔ7 (PART 1): USING ♭7 TO 3 TO MOVE FROM CHORD TO CHORD 93

Lesson Plan 18: Hearing ♭7 to 3 on II–7 | V7 | IΔ7 93

Lesson Plan 19: Using ♭7 to 3 to Improvise on II–7 | V7 94

Lesson Plan 20: Using ♭7 to 3 to Improvise on V7 | IΔ7 96

Lesson Plan 21: Using ♭7 to 3 to Improvise on II–7 | V7 | IΔ7 98

Teacher's Notes 99
- Singing Backgrounds 99
- Tips for Building 8th-Note Lines 99
- Rhythm Section 100
  - Piano/Guitar: Using Stepwise Motion 100

CHAPTER 13   II–7 | V7 | I (PART TWO): MELODIC ARPEGGIOS AND DOMINANT CYCLES   101

Lesson Plan 22: Towards Improvising on II–7 | V7 | IΔ7   101
Lesson Plan 23: Introducing ♯9 and ♭9 on the V7 Chord   102
Lesson Plan 24: Dominant Cycles (Part 1): 1-2-3-5 and 1-5-3-5   103
Lesson Plan 25: Dominant Cycles (Part 2): 3-5-7-9 Arpeggios   105
Lesson Plan 26: Dominant Cycles (Part 3): Adding and Dropping Beats   107
Lesson Plan 27: 3-5-7-9 + Approach Tones: Dropping and Adding Beats on II–7 | V7 | IΔ7   110

CHAPTER 14   PLAYING THE BLUES (PART 1)   113

Why We Didn't Start with the Blues   113
What the Blues Means to Us   113
Lesson Plan 28: Using Approach Tones to Hear the Harmonic Form of the Blues (Less Advanced)   115
Lesson Plan 29: 1-2-3-5 on the Blues (Less Advanced)   120
Teacher's Notes   123
    Harmonic Options on the Blues   123
    The Turnaround   123
    Rhythm Section   124
      Piano: An Example of Comping on the Blues   124

CHAPTER 15   THE VOCAL FORM OF THE BLUES   125

Lesson Plan 30: Introducing the Vocal Form of the Blues (Less Advanced)   125
Lesson Plan 31: Instrumental Blues (Part 1—Less Advanced)   127
Lesson Plan 32: Instrumental Blues (Part 2—Less Advanced)   129
Lesson Plan 33: Instrumental Blues (Part 3—More Advanced)   131
List of Blues Tunes   132
Teacher's Notes   133
    Rhythm Section   133
      Recommended Blues Tracks for Piano   133

CHAPTER 16   A GUIDE TO TRANSCRIBING (LEARNING BY EAR)   135

Getting Started   135
Make It Their Own   136
A Few Examples of Creative Practice Inspired by Transcribing   137

CHAPTER 17   THE BENEFITS OF PLAY: WHY WE TEACH JAZZ   141

A Word about a Word: *Play*   141
The Effects of Jazz: Talking Points for Admin and Parents   142

APPENDIX: JAZZ CHORD SYMBOLS   145

INDEX   151

PREFACE

This book began with a conversation that turned my teaching world upside down. I had studied with John McNeil for a year as a student at the New England Conservatory of Music. On a whim, I found myself knocking at his door.

Me: John, we need to talk about your teaching.
John: Oh! Teaching is easy!
Me: (stunned) Easy? What do you mean, easy?
John: Well, everybody learns the same way—exposure and repetition.
Me: Okay. Let's say I'm willing to accept that. When you're teaching jazz, how do you get your students to engage repetition creatively?
John: Simple. *You just have be sure that they're making choices all the time while they practice.*

He said it like it was the most obvious thing in the world. I later learned that the "exposure and repetition" piece was a Carmine Caruso axiom. (John studied with Carmine for years.) But John's idea—of students making choices all the time while practicing—felt revolutionary to me. And my teaching, in every genre, has been trying to catch up since.

I can't help but remember one other pivotal conversation; this time as a graduate student at Arizona State University, where I was pursuing a Master's degree in classical trumpet with Dave Hickman. At the time, the great Sam Pilafian (tuba artist extraordinaire) was also on faculty.

Sam's coaching was unparalleled. He embodied simplicity, with an uncanny knack to create conditions for students to bump into the edge of their abilities, over and over, without flooding them. Then, with a few perfectly timed words or gestures from Sam, the student would find themselves, a touch bewildered, on the other side of the proverbial wall, new skill in hand.

Simple. Direct. Imaginative. Watching Sam teach was watching art. He was a master.

In my second year at ASU, another whim came up inside. This time, I found myself knocking on Sam's office door. He answered, and I stumbled over my words as I tried to express how much I loved jazz, how I wanted to learn to *really* play it. I asked him who I should study with. Honestly, I fully wondered if Sam would offer to teach me himself.

He didn't bat an eye: "Man, if you *really* want to figure this music out, you have to get with John McNeil."

Thanks, Sam.

—Ryan Nielsen, Utah, Home of the Jazz (thanks for that one, Delfeayo), 2022

ACKNOWLEDGMENTS

This book began in 2010 and has benefitted from the thoughtful insights of so many people. A special thanks to Becky Roesler, Ben Mathews, Nathan Royal, Kate Skinner, Holly Nielsen, Robert Sears, Mark Watkins, Jeff Lovell, Aaron Miller, Justin Nielsen, Jon Armstrong, Kobie Watkins, Farayi Malek, Elaine Nielsen, Kendell Nielsen, Newell Dayley, Diane Soelberg, and Bryce Mecham.

CHAPTER 1

GETTING STARTED

Teaching jazz improvisation is easier than you think. You don't have to be a jazz expert to give your students (or yourself) a solid foundation in jazz improvisation. The demands placed on modern music educators are immense and, quite simply, not fair. Often, one person is hired to run an entire program: teach all the instruments, be a competent conductor, teach Western classical music, run the marching band and pep band (expected), perhaps organize a community band, and teach jazz by running a big band and maybe a couple of small groups. Somehow, you're supposed to teach your students to improvise as well.

We can't help with all of the above, but this book contains a simple and effective way to teach or learn jazz improvisation. With our lesson plans, improvisation can be taught during rehearsal, in the classroom or privately. They are designed to help your students feel success early on and keep them excited about learning.

Everyone Can Improvise

Given sufficient exposure and repetition, anyone can learn to improvise in music as successfully as they improvise in life. We are all born with the ability to improvise; the human brain is wired for it. We deal with many of the challenges in life by improvising in some form or another; it's how we cope with the unexpected and is part of being human. It's a natural process—like breathing or walking on uneven ground. Unfortunately, many believe that jazz improvisation is mysterious and only a select few can find their way. This leads to the false belief that you either have the ability or you don't. This simply isn't true. Yes, there are teaching methods that make learning jazz seem as difficult as learning chemistry or physics, but it's not. Regardless of how it might seem, it's just music. Like all music, it takes practice . . . but that doesn't mean it's difficult. Approached the right way, becoming a jazz musician is a straightforward process.

Training the Subconscious to Make Choices

The difference between playing a written solo and an improvised one is obvious: an improvised solo is made up on the spot and a written one has been composed in advance. Improvising requires us to make choices on the spot.

This is an important point; it tells us that someone learning to improvise has to develop skill in making choices, and very, very quickly at that. Only the subconscious can do that fast enough to improvise effectively (the conscious mind is just too slow).*

The subconscious has instant access to everything we know. It offers more creativity and variety than the conscious mind and is extremely powerful. The bottom line is that the conscious mind is just too slow. For these reasons, when we teach improvisation, our primary goal is to train the subconscious to help make creative choices, right from the start. To effectively involve the subconscious, you need to know that it operates according to definite rules. For starters, there's one way in which the subconscious behaves like a very literal four-year-old: it must be *shown* what you want it to learn; you can't just tell it what to do. This means that to incorporate new information while improvising, you must show that information to the subconscious *a number of times and in different musical situations*. Otherwise, it just won't stick.

Beyond Rote Memory

We turned a corner in our teaching when we realized that the brain wires itself differently for improvising than it does for rote memory.[†]

Before we realized this, our teaching mirrored much of what we saw in jazz education—rote memorization of patterns and licks. On the one hand, patterns are indispensable for learning to visualize and for training the ear to recognize changes in chord quality, root movement, unfamiliar harmonic concepts, and the effect of a strongly constructed line. On the other hand, cobbling together memorized patterns is not improvising.

The facts are:

1) Rote practice stores information in the brain in one way.
2) Practice that demands choice—any choice at all—stores information in a different way.[‡]

Clearly, what is needed is skill in making choices.

We all learn by doing. As you guide your students through the materials in this book, *let your students experience sounds **before** you put names to them. If they do this, understanding will come a lot quicker.* This is very important. When we don't let students hear, sing, and play sounds *before* placing names on them, they think that the name is what matters.

How to Use This Book

It would be best to read the whole book if your schedule allows. If you don't have time to read it all, *begin with **chapters 2**, **3**, and **11**, in that order*. Then, check out the lesson plans in **chapters 14** and **15** that are labeled "Less Advanced."

---

* Some may argue that it's possible to improvise with your conscious mind. They will say that what they're doing is thinking of things to play, and then playing them. Actually, it only seems like they are consciously thinking of what to play. In reality, the subconscious chooses or constructs a musical idea, then hands it up to your conscious mind and goes back to work making something else. If you find a musical phrase lying on the floor of your conscious mind, you're apt to think that you had something to do with its creation.
† If interested, check out Charles Limb's TED-Ed presentation, "Your Brain on Improv."
‡ We know this implies that information storage in the brain is a clear-cut process. It's not. It's far more complex, with boundaries that are not always clear. For our purposes, however, this is a useful model.

Chapters 2 and **3** show you how to start your students. They are the foundation for everything that follows. **Chapter 11** simplifies jazz chord symbols. **Chapters 14** and **15** introduce the blues. *We strongly recommend that you introduce the less-advanced lesson plans in the blues **chapter 15** after completing **chapter 3**.*

LESSON PLANS FOR CHAPTERS 2–10, 12–13, 15–16

Each lesson plan introduces a new skill or two. We recommend practicing each exercise in two or three keys, depending on your repertoire and student needs. Eventually, you want your students playing in at least a half-dozen keys, but not yet. Every lesson plan begins with a track for recommended listening; these are like essential building blocks for your students' jazz DNA and may well be the most important part of the session. Every one of those tracks will almost certainly be music they would otherwise not hear.

Sometimes, you may well spend several sessions on one lesson plan. When this is the case, feel free to choose from the following list of albums for further listening:

Art Blakey and the Jazz Messengers, *Free for All*
Art Blakey and the Jazz Messengers, *A Night at Birdland (Vol. 1 and 2)*
Clifford Brown, *Study in Brown*
Clifford Brown, *More Study in Brown*
The Clifford Brown-Max Roach Quintet, *More Live at the Bee Hive*
John Coltrane, *Blue Train*
John Coltrane, *Giant Steps*
John Coltrane, *Coltrane Plays the Blues*
Chick Corea, *Now He Sings, Now He Sobs*
Miles Davis, *My Funny Valentine*
Miles Davis, *Cookin'*
Miles Davis, *Relaxin'*
Miles Davis, *Someday My Prince Will Come*
Miles Davis, *Miles Smiles*
Miles Davis, *ESP*
Miles Davis, *Live at the Plugged Nickel*
Bill Evans, *Interplay*
Joe Henderson, *In 'n Out*
Joe Henderson, *Inner Urge*
Freddie Hubbard, *Ready for Freddie*
Freddie Hubbard, *Hub-Tones*
Elvin Jones, *Live at the Lighthouse*
Oscar Peterson Trio (featuring Clark Terry), *Oscar Peterson Trio + One*
Sonny Rollins, *Way Out West*
Sonny Rollins, *Saxophone Colossus*
Sonny Rollins (with John Coltrane), *Tenor Madness*
Sonny Rollins, *Sonny Rollins Plus Four*
Shirley Scott, *Soul Shoutin'*
Shirley Scott, *Great Scott*
Horace Silver, *Cape Verdean Blues*
Horace Silver, *Song for My Father*

Horace Silver, *Blowin' the Blues Away*
Larry Young, *Unity*

In **chapters 2–7**, there are scale drills at the beginning of each lesson plan. These drills may appear to be unrelated to the lesson plan, but they lay the groundwork for **chapter 8**. Do not skip them. **Chapter 8** will be very challenging if your students haven't done the preparatory work.

We made the lesson plans as concise as we could, and they should need little explanation. As we said before, *emphasize doing rather than talking*. The fewer words said, the better. If your students are doing what you want them to do, they're learning what you want them to learn. We recommend a ratio of fifty minutes playing for every ten minutes talking. If you need to explain something, keep things simple and non-technical. Avoid jargon at all costs.

Unless specifically stated otherwise, teach each step of every lesson plan by call and response. You sing and/or play; they sing and/or play. Get them used to memorizing things right on the spot. They'll get good at it! They really will! Wait until they've tried several times before giving in to the urge write things on the board. If all you do is get your students playing the material in **chapters 2** and **3**, they will be light years ahead of what we usually hear from middle school and high school students (and many college students we've heard, for that matter).

There are Teacher's Notes at the end of each chapter. These notes include all of the information we present about teaching the rhythm section (Bass, Drums, Piano/Keyboard, Guitar).

APPENDICES

There is an appendix at the back of the book which we believe will be extremely useful to you: a Guide to Chord Symbols.

HARMONIC CONCEPTS

If you want to get young people improvising, you can't cover everything. In our experience, the learning process gets watered down when we spread the students' attention too thin. To this end, we purposely left out some harmonic concepts that are commonly used in jazz, such as the diminished scale, the harmonic minor scale, or any polytonality. We also don't introduce the pentatonic scale, although the blues scale almost qualifies as one. There are more than enough harmonic concepts in this book to build interesting solos, and many famous jazz solos use only the materials we're presenting.

Tips for Getting Started

Sometimes educators feel enormous pressure to be jazz experts before they can teach it. They may even feel a touch insecure about teaching jazz. We hereby give you permission to not feel any pressure at all. If you don't have the answer to a particular question, or just don't feel well-enough versed in jazz to teach it, relax. You're not alone in this—we're just an e-mail away. It's okay to not know things in front of your students. We do it regularly. Even if jazz doesn't feel like home base, you are the expert in the room when it comes to music, and your musicianship will support your students as you all develop together. Values such as thematic unity, variety, opposition, balance, and expression all apply to jazz, just as in other musical styles. So, if jazz is a new musical language to you, don't worry if you have an accent or if your vocabulary is limited. Just keep at it.

Please adapt the lesson plans to reflect your personal teaching style. These lesson plans don't require anything more than the usual whiteboard/smartboard/tablet, a way to play recordings for the class, and maybe an extra piano keyboard for the teacher.

Our lesson plans are designed so that you can easily hit the pause button and return as needed. This allows you the flexibility to devote a certain percentage of your rehearsal/class time to these topics. Dedicating 30 percent (or more) of class time to improvising would be a good place to start. If that's not possible, something is always better than nothing. The important thing is for your students to touch base with improvisation as often as possible.

INCORPORATING RHYTHM

The body and mind coordinate themselves more efficiently if you give them a *consistent* time frame in which to operate. In jazz, this is absolute law. What's more, it doesn't matter how slow a tempo is, as long as it's *steady*! Repeat: it doesn't matter how slow a tempo is, as long as it's *steady*!

We strongly recommend using a loud metronome or an app that can be amplified. When your class first explores an exercise, play it rubato to give everyone enough time to hear and feel the pitches, their relationship to one another and the underlying harmony. Very soon, however, the class will be playing in tempo and will benefit from a steady timekeeping device to maintain order.

It's important to hear the metronome clicks as the 2nd and 4th beats of each bar to make sure these beats are emphasized. Hearing this may take some effort, certainly by the students and possibly by yourself. Don't give up on it, though.

Reconsidering Beginning with the Blues

The blues is not just a part of jazz, it makes jazz what it is. In spite of this, we feel it may not be the best place to start teaching students to improvise. We recognize that we are breaking with a time-honored tradition in saying this, and we mean no disrespect. To the contrary, whenever we hear someone say, "It's just a blues," we know they don't understand jazz. To us, that's kind of like saying of a painting, "It's just a Rembrandt."

Really playing a blues means really playing jazz. However, students who start with the blues scale are typically unfamiliar with how jazz musicians *actually play* on a blues. As a result, they usually run up and down the blues scale without regard to the sounds that make the blues a blues. In short, we think that the blues is too important a part of jazz to be treated this way.

If you prefer to start with the blues, be our guest. You might consider starting with **chapters 14** and **15**. Although most of what we do in those chapters depends on earlier chapters, we designed this book to support what you feel your students need. Use it as you see fit.

If you're getting pressure from peers or supervisors to teach kids the blues, dip into **chapters 14** and **15** from time to time (see the lesson plans labeled "Less Advanced"). After you do that, they're still going to have to come back and learn the basics as they unfold from **chapters 2–10**. We don't approach the blues like the default kiddie-version of jazz. Charlie Parker and other innovators helped it evolve way beyond that.

Instead of starting with blues, we begin with the sound of Dorian minor. (Crucial note: *in jazz the default minor is Dorian.* In our experience as professional jazz musicians, this is overwhelmingly the case.) We used to think that our students could start by improvising on entire scales and get somewhere, but that didn't actually work. They ended up treating all the notes equally, and didn't play anything harmonically specific or melodically strong. Eventually they have to learn to hear and play structures, and it's actually *easier* to start off that way. Improvising with structures in the scale (such as thirds, triads or 7th-chords) usually results in stronger lines and more interesting melodic shapes.

Now, time to get started. From our point of view, this kind of teaching is rarely tried, but we've seen that it's more effective. It doesn't leave anyone behind, and if you have advanced students, they'll be challenged as well. In fact, in our own practice, we regularly return to versions of the basic skills and concepts in this book. In many ways, this book is our answer to the question, "What did the musicians we admire practice?" We're giving students a place to start; a direction which should inexorably lead them to being the type of player that they admire. There's no question about it. When they ask, "What kind of disciplines did these artists go through that allowed them to play these things?" you can safely say that it's the type of things that we put forth in this book. Did those artists practice things that are more advanced than the contents found in this book? Yes. But your students will eventually arrive at that too, if they follow the basic principles we present here. We've done our best to give the students a creative experience right from the start.

And remember, as questions come up, we're just an email away: john@mcneiljazz.com, ryan@ryanstrumpet.com.

CHAPTER 2

BASIC CONCEPTS

The Root Triad and Jazz Rhythms

Before getting to the first lesson plan, you need to understand the way jazz musicians think about the relationship between chords and scales, and how to read and write jazz chord symbols. If you're already comfortable with this information, go straight to Lesson Plan 1. Otherwise, continue reading.

Chord Versus Scale

In jazz, we often think of a chord and a scale as the same thing: a set of pitches that, taken together, make a sound. Below is an example. You can see that the seven pitches in a D minor chord that extends to the 13th are the same seven pitches in a D Dorian scale. The only difference between the two is that the scale is seven tones played one at a time in order, and the chord is the same seven tones separated by thirds and played all at once. Sometimes we use the term chord/scale. It's easy to see why.

Taken together, these seven pitches completely *define* the sound of a D minor chord. For this reason, we refer to them as *defining pitches*.

Reading Jazz Chord Symbols

In jazz the chord symbol automatically implies all of the notes in the defining scale. There are usually three parts to each chord symbol: **root**, **quality**, and **extension.**

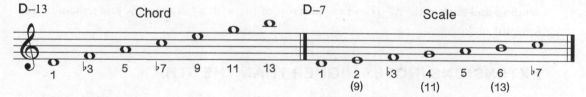

ROOT

The letter at the beginning of the chord symbol tells you the root of the chord. If your training is largely in classical theory, this is where you will most likely misread a jazz chord symbol: *the case (upper or lower) of the root does NOT indicate quality.* Upper case does NOT mean major, and lower case does NOT mean minor. In the above example, the root is 'C.'

QUALITY

The middle of the chord symbol tells you the quality of the chord. Is it major? Minor? Half-diminished? Look to the middle for chord quality. In the above example, the quality is labeled as "maj," which means major.

MINOR

We use the minus symbol for minor (i.e., "–"). For example, F–7 means F minor. We know we've said it already, but here it is again: in jazz, the default minor is *always* Dorian, NOT natural minor (Aeolian).

Note: students who have already learned their minor scales may habitually play ♭6 on a minor chord (this is especially problematic on a II–7 chord). If so, it's likely because they don't hear the difference between the two. To correct this, have them sing the basic root triad plus a flat 6, and then the basic root triad plus the raised 6th, side by side. Differences which at first seem very small will loom large by simply going back and forth between the two.

MAJOR

We use the "Δ" symbol to indicate major. For example, FΔ7 means F major. You will also see major chords written with a 6 or 6/9 in the music you perform. We're going to ignore those symbols and stick with "Δ." If you come across music with a C6 or C6/9, just remember that it means major.*

EXTENSIONS (NOTES HIGHER THAN THE 5TH)

This term refers to the number (or numbers) at the end of the chord symbol, which tell you how far to stack the thirds in the chord (to the 7th, 9th, 11th, or 13th). But here's the thing: every chord symbol implies a full chord/scale (usually seven notes), *no matter which number is written as the extension.* For example, even if the chord symbol were D–7 rather than D–13, the improviser would still understand the defining pitches of the chord in the same way—as all seven notes in the D Dorian scale.

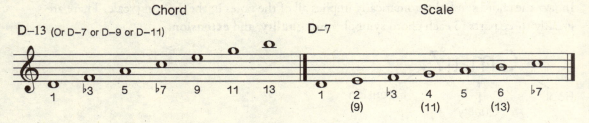

---

* In jazz you find instances like this, primarily because the music wasn't codified until years after the fact. It's one of those things you just have to accept and get used to.

EXCEPTIONS TO THE THREE-PART CHORD SYMBOL

The biggest exception to the three-part chord symbol is the dominant chord symbol, which only has the root name followed by the extension (for example, C7). Jazz is not completely consistent in its notation; you will see dominant chord symbols written as C7, C9, or C13. Even so, we only use the number "7" (i.e., C7) in this book.

For more information on chord symbols as they relate to scale qualities, see the appendix at the back of the book. You will also find Chapter 11 very useful.

Lesson Plan 1: Improvising on the Root Triad

Every lesson plan has examples of what to do, and you'll notice that the lesson plans don't have a lot of explanation. In fact, especially with younger students, explaining often gets in the way. This is worth repeating from Chapter 1: Students learn by doing. Don't talk too much or give long explanations. *Let your students experience sounds before you put names on them.* Get your students *doing* what's in the lesson plan, and they will improve quickly.

Reminder: Unless stated otherwise, teach each step of every lesson plan by call and response. You sing and/or play; they sing and/or play.

Do not skip the scale drills **at the beginning of each lesson plan. They will prepare your students for Chapter 8. Let's get started!**

Each lesson plan will include a "Recommended Recording" for you to have playing while your students get set up for class/rehearsal.

RECOMMENDED RECORDING, LESSON PLAN 1: ART BLAKEY, *UGETSU*. Recommended track: "One by One."

1. Write the D Dorian scale in whole notes on the board like this:

Again, no need to explain what it is yet, or what it's called, or why. Avoid jargon and just write it out and have your students sing and play it (see step 2). If you have B♭ and E♭ instruments in the room and your students are new to transposing, you may consider writing the scale in their keys as well (E Dorian and B Dorian, respectively).

2. Have your students sing and play the concert D Dorian scale up to the 9th like this:

Sing everything before you play it. This might be a hard sell, so start by having the whole class sing at once. Before you have individuals sing, consider dividing the class into groups of three or four and have each group sing by itself.

Make sure that students who are shy or have pitch trouble are teamed with stronger singers. Those who really want to play will eventually have to be able to sing everything they practice. *If they can't sing it they don't really hear it*, and if they don't hear it they will always struggle to be accurate.

3. Have your students sing and play the root triad up and down:

After playing these three notes, you might point out that this grouping is called a *triad*, and this particular triad defines the minor quality of the chord/scale more than other pitches.

4. Have them sing and play the D Dorian scale from step 2 followed by the D minor triad from step 3.

Your students need to realize that the triad comes from the scale, but more important, they have to *hear it within the scale*. Singing and playing the scale and triad side by side is the simplest way to accomplish this. This is an excellent warm-up exercise, especially when done with several Dorian scales. Right now, we are only dealing with one scale, but we will add more as your students develop. Return to it regularly, and your students will see and hear that the root triad comes from the scale.†

5. Picture two D minor triads stacked on top of each other. Sing and play through them until your students feel familiar and comfortable. If necessary, write the figure out, then erase it as they improve.

Your students will eventually improvise with these six notes, and they need to be able to see and hear stacked triads in their minds. Our students often have difficulty picturing the root triad an octave above, so form that habit early. To help them see that the upper triad also comes from the scale, it may be helpful to play the first five notes of the scale in each octave, and then play the triads.

If range is an issue, simply move the top notes down two octaves. See the Teacher's Notes at the end of this chapter for a more detailed explanation.

---

† If your students don't have the technical ability to play the full scale, start with the first three notes (D-E-F), then four (D-E-F-G), then five, and so on.

6. Randomly choose four tones from the two-triad stack. Have the students help you arrange the tones into simple melodic shapes, like this:

Sing and play each melodic shape slowly at first with a rubato feel. The more expressive you are with each shape, the more likely the new information will stick. It's important that the students make up some shapes of their own. Try conducting one note at a time, using crescendos and decrescendos and an occasional staccato note to make the shapes as interesting as possible and make it so the students have to follow your conducting (for more clarity, see the example provided in step 7 below).

7. Pick four notes out of the two-octave stack, and have each student improvise with just those four.‡

Focus on playing with expression without being confined within a tempo. Eventually your students will be playing in a tempo, but for now it's good to get the creative juices flowing without any rhythmic barriers. They can change the order and length of the notes and choose whatever expressive elements they wish. For example:

As you can see, your students have a lot of choices in addition to the pitches to sing/play: long or short, loud or soft, crescendos or decrescendos, repeated notes, rips, rapid changes in volume, and numerous things that are not in the above example, such as glissandi, growls, falls, flutter tongues, and anything else that gets your students making creative choices within

---

‡ If some students object to only having four notes to work with, simply tell them that it's easier with more notes but the point is to see how much you can do with only a few notes. Try to stoke the competitive fires when necessary.

the limits of the triad. *Most importantly, this should be fun and non-judgmental right from the start.*

At first, your students will likely be self-conscious. A remedy for this is to have the entire class play backgrounds while the soloist is playing. This is much easier to do than it may sound, and it will reinforce the sound of the triad in everyone's ears.

HOW TO CREATE A BACKGROUND

Have each student pick any note in the triad, then give them cues to indicate dynamics. Use mostly sustained chords and an occasional short one. We recommend rehearsing backgrounds *without* a soloist at first. Involving the rest of the class like this gives each soloist the safety of anonymity; they won't feel as exposed if everyone else is playing.

RHYTHM SECTION

Have the bass or piano sustain the root of the chord in the low register at all times; your students need to hear how the melody relates to the root. If the pianist is playing the root in the left hand, make sure they also play the melodic shapes with the right hand.

If your rhythm section is inexperienced, we've included information in the Teacher's Notes at the end of this chapter to help you get them started. Just look for the "Rhythm Section" heading.

Lesson Plan 2: Adding Rhythm

RECOMMENDED RECORDING, LESSON PLAN 2: ART BLAKEY, *UGETSU*. Recommended track: "On the Ginza."

1. Have the class sing and play the following scale and triad together (from Lesson Plan 1).

2. Remind them to picture, sing, and play two D minor triads stacked on top of each other. You might write it on the board again.

3. As before, randomly choose four tones from the two-triad stack. Have the students help you arrange the tones into simple melodic shapes. Here are some more examples:

Remember, if the range is too high, adjust as needed. There are recommendations for addressing range in the Teacher's Notes at the end of this chapter.

4. Choose one of the following rhythms. Create a triad shape (as in step 3) and make it fit the rhythm you have chosen (see the following examples). *Now's the time to start using a metronome clicking on beats two and four!*

Here are some examples of combining the rhythms with triad shapes:

If changing notes that often is too difficult, play some repeated notes. For example:

As you listen to recordings together as a class, notice that the 8th-notes are "swung." Listen for the fact that swung 8th-notes are neither straight nor triplet-ized. They fall somewhere in between. The music of Dexter Gordon, Freddie Hubbard, Sonny Rollins, Early Miles Davis, Art Blakey, Art Farmer, and Melba Liston are great places to start listening for jazz style. You might alternate between listening to short excerpts together and playing these rhythms together.

5. Choose one of the rhythms. Have your students sing and play it repeatedly while choosing to play different notes from the triad-stack. Now they're improvising! We recommend starting with just one chord. For example:

Make it easy. If changing pitches on each note of the rhythm feels like too much, limit the number of notes they use to one or two pitches. Adjust as needed to make sure your students experience success early on.

Fear of failure stands alone as the single greatest barrier to learning. By simplifying tasks that feel too complex, your students will gain confidence in their ability to improve.

The great teacher Carmine Caruso understood fear of learning. Carmine believed in de-constructing a hard task into a few easy tasks, and then combining them. He was fond of telling his students, "It's quicker to learn something simple than something complex." He also said, "Go back far enough, and you can always find a place for them to start." Simplify as needed.

6. Repeat steps 1 through 5 on a new chord (we recommend F–7). Write the F Dorian scale and root triad in whole notes on the board. Run through all of the exercises with the new pitches. This may take as long as it did the first time, but future scale additions will start to take less and less time. When ready, alternate between D–7 and F–7, using one basic rhythm from step 4, repeated. For example:

In this example, it's easy to see that the 3rd of F–7 (the A♭) is the only note in the F minor triad that is not in the D Dorian scale. For this reason, the A♭ is the most interesting note to play when changing to the F–7 chord. Point this out to your students.

When we introduce students to changing from one chord to another, we use minor chords that are a minor third apart, such as D–7 going to F–7. They are different enough from each other that your students will hear and feel the change as they play each one. And, because they have two common tones, they are relatively simple to visualize.

8. Have your students improvise, using *two* of the basic jazz rhythms from step 4 while choosing different notes from the triad-stack.

Repeat the first rhythm you choose once or twice, and then choose another. By doing this, students learn repetition and variation. The goal is to *randomize when they choose certain rhythms*. For example:

In this example, *rhythm 5 sounds interesting because we repeated rhythm 4 first*. Point this out to your students. It's difficult to hold more than two rhythms in your mind at the same time, especially for less experienced students. Feel free to try three rhythms, but two might be the limit.

Teacher's Notes

WHY START WITH THE TRIAD?

To improvise effectively on a scale, students need to identify the overall sound of the scale *and* hear the root triad as its center of gravity. If students begin improvising using the entire scale, they will probably use every note in the scale equally, which makes their lines wander and lack harmonic clarity. Limiting students to the root triad also teaches them economy—making musical statements without playing a lot of notes.

CHOOSING CHORDS TO BEGIN WITH

There are two ways to create your curriculum for learning different chords: 1) use our recommended sequence, or 2) practice chords directly from the repertoire you are learning. Should you choose the latter, consult Chapter 11 immediately.

Here is our recommended sequence:

1. Chord/scales a minor third apart as in the lesson plan (i.e., D–7 and F–7).
2. Chord/scales a major third apart (i.e., D–7, F♯–7).
3. Chord/scales a half step apart (i.e., D–7, E♭–7; or D–7, C♯–7).
4. Chord/scales descending in whole steps (i.e., D–7, C–7).
5. Chord/scales a tritone apart (i.e., D–7, A♭–7).

You can do this sequence starting with any minor chord. (And remember, in jazz, minor is Dorian, unless specified otherwise!)

ADJUSTING RANGE

If range is a factor, move the top one or two notes of the structure to a more comfortable register. For example:

Don't give a complicated explanation; say something like, "That sounds pretty high. Let's take the top note and put it down here. It's all the same."

DESIGNING RHYTHM

To those new to jazz, the rhythms can feel odd. The seven rhythms in Lesson Plan 2 are designed to get your students inside the jazz language quickly. These rhythms don't even scratch the surface; they're just a starting point. There are more rhythms in later lessons.

Let your students make up their own rhythms early on. Effective solo lines depend on rhythms that create momentum, and this requires syncopation (substituting an upbeat for a downbeat).

At first, most students will try to create rhythms with a lot of downbeats. If they play a rhythm that sounds like a Sousa March instead of jazz, you can modify it by adding syncopation to the beginning or end of the phrase. For example:

Less Effective Rhythm (All Downbeats)

More Effective Rhythm/Syncopated Version

In the second, stronger example, beat 1 in the first bar is an 8th-note later; in the second bar, beat 1 is an 8th-note earlier. Small adjustments like this will usually make your students' ideas more effective. Make the message, "Your idea is strong, but we can make it even stronger with one small change." Of course, if their idea wasn't strong, don't lie to them. Just say, "Let's try again."

RHYTHM SECTION

General Tips

Rhythm section players have double duty: accompanying and soloing. The lesson plans above deal with soloing, so what follows is a simple curriculum to begin learning the art of accompaniment (what jazz musicians call "comping"). *This is by no means exhaustive.* Nor is it meant to replace the many fine volumes and recordings devoted to the art of comping. Rather, this is a jump start to give you, the educator, a clear direction for mentoring your students.

To learn both soloing and comping, students in the rhythm section should go back and forth between the melodic lines from the lesson plans (above) and comping (which we describe below). The rhythm section's most important job is to provide harmony and rhythmic groove (to us, a groove is a distinct rhythmic feel created by a set of repeated rhythms). Eventually, you want the rhythm section to interact with the soloists by composing musical compliments to the ideas played. However, they can't be expected to interact until they have a basic command of the material.

Any time you are working on rhythmic concepts with your rhythm section, remember to use a metronome clicking on beats two and four. Help them get to the point where they can tell if their sense of time is earlier or later than the metronome. A steady pulse is paramount.

It's not only okay to use class time for listening, it's necessary. If you try to apply the information in this book without listening to the music, it's like trying to speak French without hearing it spoken.

Piano: Basic Voicings

The question we get asked most often by our fellow educators is how to voice chords at the piano. To this end, here is a simple curriculum.

What follows are four distinct steps for your pianist to learn how to voice chords. Start with step 1, apply it to the chords you need, and gradually move through the other steps as your pianist matures.

1. Start by playing *roots in the left hand* while playing the *3rd and 7th in the right hand*:

The lowest note in the right hand can be either the 3rd or the 7th (as above).

2. Left hand only: Have the piano play the *3rd and 7th in the left hand* while the bass plays the root.

3. Left hand: Add the 5th and the 9th to the voicings in step 2. There are four ways this can be done. Practice all four.

The basic 3rd and 7th are still part of these voicings; we just added the 5th and 9th.

Every voicing doesn't work in every register. Trust your ears. As a general rule, stay between third-line D (bass clef) for the bottom note of the voicing and C above middle C for the top note. If a student plays a voicing that's too low, you will immediately hear that it is muddy. To help them hear the lack of clarity, play the muddy voicing (too low) and a clear one, side by side.

4. Play four-note voicings with the 3rd and 7th in the left hand, and the 5th and 9th in the right hand. There are two ways to do this (for now):

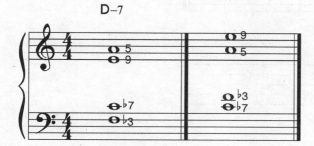

To add rhythm to their comping, use the same rhythms we provided in Lesson Plan 2. For example:

You can combine rhythm with any of the voicings we've shown you. If your pianist is more advanced, they can change their voicing on each note of the rhythm.

Once your pianist has basic command of this material, begin teaching them to interact with the soloist or ensemble. They have two options while comping: 1) play at the same time as the soloist/ensemble, or 2) play in the spaces (when the soloist/ensemble are sustaining a long note or resting).

The listener can only listen to one thing at a time. If I'm talking and you're talking, people listening will have to shut down one to understand the other. The same is true in music. As such, rhythmic complexity in comping is more effective if it doesn't interfere with the soloist or the band. Have your comping instruments play busier rhythms when the soloist plays rests or sustained notes.

There is much, much more to the world of comping than we should realistically get into here. We highly recommend Mark Levine's *Jazz Piano Book* and Luke Gillespie's *Stylistic II/ V7/I Voicings for Keyboardists* for further study.

Guitar: Basic Voicings

Guitar voicings are different from piano voicings to some degree because students often memorize shapes on the fretboard rather than thinking about individual notes. Still, the principles we talked about for the piano can be an effective place to start for the guitar as well.

1. Play the root, 3rd, and 7th.

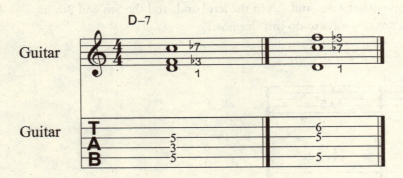

2. 2-note voicings: play the 3rd and 7th by themselves (while the bass plays the root).

3. 3-note voicings: Add a third note to the 2-note voicing. If the 3rd is on the bottom, add the 9th; if the 7th is on the bottom, add the 5th.

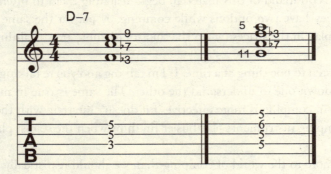

Note that there's a G added on the bottom of the second voicing (above). This lies very well on the guitar and is a well-known modal minor sound. You can hear it on Miles Davis's "So What" from the *Kind of Blue* album.

4. 4-note voicings: just as with the piano, play 3 and 7; 5 and 9.

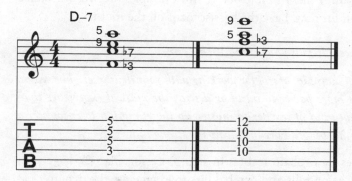

Important: All of the same rhythmic and comping principles we discussed with the piano apply to the guitar.

When comping, young guitarists tend to play more downbeats than young piano players. It probably feels natural because they've done it so much in rock and pop bands. At any rate, do your best to have them comp rhythms that have a lot of upbeats (start a half beat early, etc.).

Bass: Walking Bass Lines with Triad Pitches

In straight-ahead jazz your bassist should focus on playing quarter notes. As in the lesson plan, they should start by choosing notes from the two-octave triad. Give them two options:

1. Place the root on the first beat of every measure. All notes should be sustained, not short and thumpy.

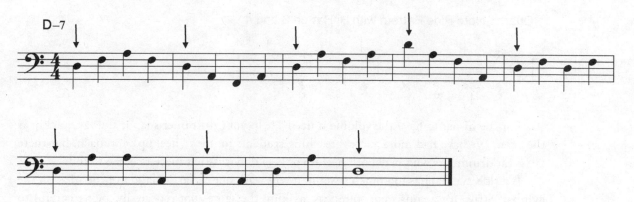

2. Place the root on the first beat of every *other* measure.

Simplify the bass line if your bass player is relatively new to the instrument. You could start them with just two notes, or limit them to one octave, for example. We will introduce more interesting bass lines later, but for now, have the bassist focus on the root triad.

Drums: Basic Ride Cymbal Technique, Hi-Hat Usage, and Kicks

You may notice that we're offering an awful lot of tips for working with your drummer. The reason for that is simple: the drummer has more power to build or destroy the musical experience than any other musician. It takes a special kind of teacher to muster up the gumption to encounter a drummer, head on, about music (of all things). Fortune favors the strong . . .

When the horns are playing shapes in a rubato feel (as in step 3, Lesson Plan 2), have your drummer play freely with mallets, using rolls and cymbal hits to exaggerate the dynamics as you conduct. We want them to get in the habit of responding to the conductor and/or soloist; they'll need that later.

Teach them that every time they strike a cymbal (as in a cymbal crash) *they must simultaneously strike a drum*, starting with the bass drum. This will reinforce technique and get them thinking about phrase shapes.

When crashing a cymbal, they should strike with the body of the stick.

Once the band is playing shapes with rhythms (Lesson Plan 2 Step 4), here is a suggested order of priorities:

1. Play ONLY quarter notes on the ride cymbal and lock it in with the bass. Strike with the tip of the drumstick. Play the hi-hat on 2 and 4. *The hi-hat should be as loud or louder than the ride cymbal.*

Quarter Note Ride Pattern with Hi-Hat on 2 and 4

For the hi-hat to have the volume it needs, help your drummer snap it shut as quickly as they can. We have had more success teaching students to use a "heel up" approach, but there are great drummers who play both heel up or heel down. What matters is the sound.

If a ride cymbal has too much sustain, it will wash out the articulation of the stick on the cymbal. Strive for a consistent sound by striking the same spot repeatedly, being careful to allow the stick to rebound off the cymbal. We recommend avoiding cymbals with rivets so that your drummer can prioritize clarity.

For examples of masterful ride cymbal playing, invite your drummer to go to YouTube and watch videos of drummers like Art Blakey, Tony Williams, Sonny Payne, Philly Joe Jones, Billy Higgins, Roy Haynes, Jimmy Cobb, Grady Tate, Tain Watts, Al Foster, Mel Lewis, Billy Hart, Elvin Jones, Gregory Hutchinson, Herlin Riley, Brian Blade, or Kobie Watkins.

Note: For now, prioritize the ride cymbal and hi-hat. The drum parts we often see for straight-ahead charts show the bass drum playing on beats 1 and 3. Don't do it. The universe hangs in the balance.

Don't let your students use the bass drum to play quarter notes (yet). At first, have them think of the bass drum as another voice. Later, they can develop the ability to "feather" the bass drum on quarter notes. ("Feather" is a term for playing the bass drum so softly that it almost can't be heard, and drummers who do it well simply enhance the front of the notes coming from the bassist.) But at first (and for some time), we recommend no bass drum on quarter notes.

2. Once the quarter note feels consistent, occasionally add upbeats to the ride pattern as pick-up notes to the next beat. For example:

Quarter Note Ride Pattern With Occasional Upbeats

We have notated the upbeats as 16th-note pickups to the next beat. We have found this to be more effective than triplets (initially), especially for younger drummers.

3. When the quarter note is well established, add the left hand on the snare only. Begin with the same rhythms the class is playing from the lesson plans while still playing the groove on the ride cymbal and hi-hat. *Make sure that adding the left hand doesn't change what's happening with the ride cymbal and hi-hat.* For example:

Rhythm 1 on Snare Combined with Ride and Hi-Hat

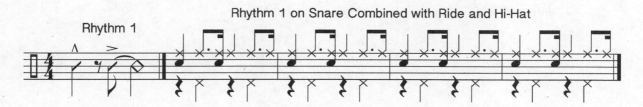

4. Once they can comfortably play these rhythms on the snare drum, alternate between the bass drum and snare to perform the rhythm. For example:

Rhythm 1 Played Between Snare and Bass Drum With Ride Pattern

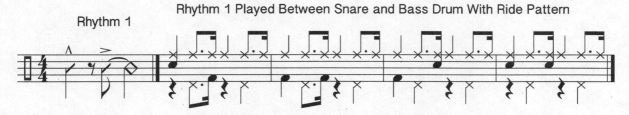

The composite rhythm is always there, it's just being played as a conversation between the snare and bass drums.

Important: teach them to match volume between the snare and bass drum; most young students have a lead foot.

The Hi-Hat

A common problem in young drummers is their approach to the standard swing pattern on the hi-hat. Too often, young drummers open the hi-hat *on* beats 1 and 3. For example:

Less Effective: Hi-Hat Opens on Downbeats

For a more effective feel, have them open on the upbeats just *before* beats 1 and 3:

More Effective: Hi-Hat Opens on Upbeats

Be careful not to have them open the hi-hat too far. The two cymbals should sizzle against each other when open in this context.

Drummer's Priorities

1. Connect with the bass.
2. Connect with the chord instruments.
3. Support the soloist and/or ensemble.

In our experience, every time the drummer loses track of these priorities *in this order*, the music suffers.

CHAPTER 3

ADDING THE 2ND (1-2-3-5)

Playing the root triad (1-3-5) by itself will eventually get boring for your students. In this chapter, we add the 2nd degree of the chord/scale (1-2-3-5).

Initially, your students need to hear and see the 2nd step of the scale *as an ornament* to the basic triad. For now, when they play the 2nd step of the scale they must move directly to 3 or 1. Soon the 2nd step will be heard as a passing or approach tone, with the root triad as the center of gravity.

Review lesson plans any time, as many times as you see fit. In fact, we recommend returning to previous lesson plans regularly. Sometimes it's better to repeat lesson plans rather than move on, especially when you introduce new chord/scales to your students' repertoire.

Lesson Plan 3: Adding the 2nd Degree

RECOMMENDED RECORDING, LESSON PLAN 3: HORACE SILVER, *BLOWIN' THE BLUES AWAY*. Recommended track: "Blowin' the Blues Away."

1. Review Lesson Plans 1 and 2. In particular, have your students repeat the Dorian scale/triad warm up (reprinted below) *on more than one scale.* Review the two-octave triad stack and a couple of rhythms (also reprinted below). *Remember to have them sing what they play!*

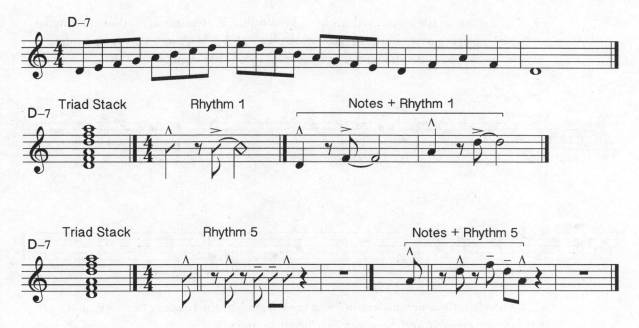

2. Now we're adding the 2nd step of the scale to the two-octave triad-stack:

Just like before, have your students create triad shapes, but now add the 2nd step of the scale to those shapes. *Remember, 2 has to move to 3 or 1.*

As before, sing and play the shapes together in a rubato feel with the rhythm section sustaining the chord. Take turns allowing each student to make up their own triad shape, adding the 2nd step of the scale at least once. Have the class sing and play each shape they create.

3. Choose one of the seven rhythms from Lesson Plan 2. Repeat the rhythm and improvise by playing notes from the triad-stack plus 2 (1-2-3-5). A very slow tempo might be necessary. Speed doesn't matter so long as it's *steady*. For example:

Remember, these are just examples; give each student the freedom to play within a range that feels comfortable and doesn't involve needless stress.

ADDING THE 2ND (1-2-3-5) 27

Repeat this step on at least two more of the basic rhythms. Here they are as a reminder:

4. Improvise, using two of the basic rhythms from step 3 while choosing notes from the triad-stack plus 2 (1-2-3-5).

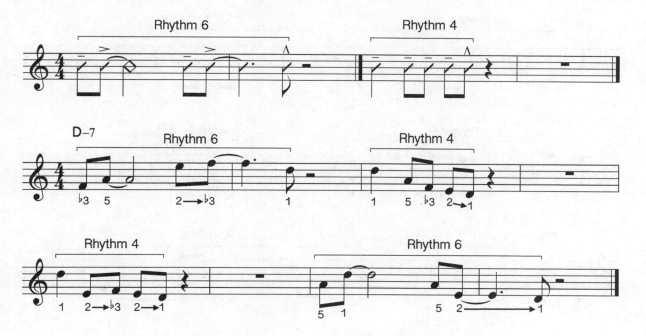

Lesson Plan 4: Building Longer 8th-Note Lines

RECOMMENDED RECORDING, LESSON PLAN 4: HORACE SILVER, *BLOWIN' THE BLUES AWAY*. Recommended track: "Sister Sadie."

Now would be a good time to regroup. As a reminder, if your students can handle the materials we have presented thus far, they will be light years ahead of what we are accustomed to hearing at high school jazz festivals and clinics. There's no need to be in a hurry.

28 THE CLASSROOM GUIDE TO JAZZ IMPROVISATION

Don't move on until everyone is at least semi-comfortable with the material from the first three lesson plans.

Continue to quickly review the scale exercises from previous lesson plans (i.e., full scale + root triad) before advancing to step 1.

1. Have the class sing and play the following scale study together:

Playing this study is necessary to prepare your students for chapter 8.

2. Review the previous lesson plan by combining 2 or 3 rhythms with 1-2-3-5 shapes (triad-stack plus 2). Remember to use a metronome to keep everyone honest.

3. Call and response. Have your students sing and play these four consecutive 8th-notes, taken from the two-octave stack of the triad plus 2 (1-2-3-5). Don't write it down; play (or sing) it for them and have them copy you.

If your students have trouble with four consecutive 8th-notes, start with three notes, or even two notes. In a short time, they'll be able to keep track of four notes. (See the Teacher's Notes at the end of the chapter for more ideas on how to simplify this step.)

4. Increase the length of the 8th-note line by adding one pick-up note chosen from the triad-stack. Have the class pick whether the note should come from below or above the first note of the original cell. (We use the term "cell" to designate the original four-note shape—see below.)

Again, don't write it out! Play it for them (or sing it). First, rubato; then do the same in tempo.

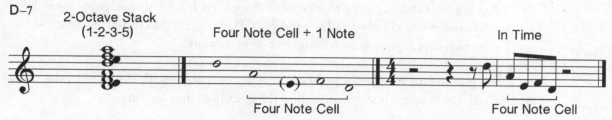

Starting with a familiar fragment and adding one note at a time, at the beginning or the end, is a near-foolproof way of developing vocabulary without undue stress.

5. Increase the length of the 8th-note line by adding another pick-up note ('F' in the example below). Again, have them choose whether the pickup is coming from above or below (either will work, so long as it comes from 1-2-3-5).

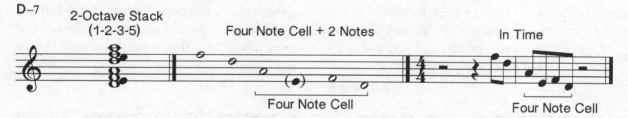

The last note of the phrase can be either long or short.

6. (Optional) If the students seem undaunted by two pickup notes, by all means add another one.

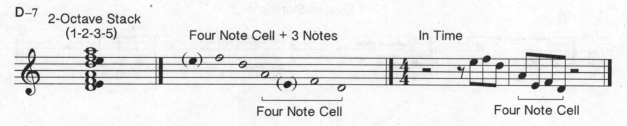

You could stop here, or continue to add notes in this way as long as you like. For now, there is no need to exceed two measures of 8th-notes.

7. Have students change the notes in the original four-note cell, and proceed to add pickup notes just like they did with the first one.

When it's easy for your students to begin with a four-note cell, try beginning with a six-note cell, gradually adding pick-ups in the same manner. This is not true improvisation; it's improvisation in slow motion. The important thing is that your students make choices in creating each new line, and that their ears become familiar with these sounds.

8. Repeat steps 3 through 7 on an F–7 chord (or another chord from the repertoire you are working on).

9. Allow students to freely improvise on triad shapes and 1-2-3-5 shapes, going back and forth between two chords (i.e., D–7 and F–7). Have the rhythm section alternate between each chord, playing each for four or eight measures.

Don't give them a lot of rules to follow. Just let them create with the material they have internalized. Don't worry if they don't follow the guidelines. Just let 'em go.

Teacher's Notes

OTHER POSSIBILITIES ON 1-2-3-5

Having 2 move to 3 or 1 trains your students to hear the root triad as the tonal center of the scale. Make sure that they understand that this is not a new sound; it is just the triad with an ornament.

After they hear the triad in this way, you can explore other possibilities on 1-2-3-5. Begin by exploring 1-2-3. We very strongly recommend teaching these to your students by call and response (you play it or sing it, they play it or sing it back). Try these same shapes on F Dorian and other scales as well.

Emphasize beginning somewhere other than the root. Make up games to get your students to make choices. For example, each student plays four notes using these three pitches; they have to do it twice, and the second time needs to be different from the first. Tell them they can repeat notes if they wish. Remember, *it's vital that they make choices right from the start.*

Once they are comfortable with 1-2-3, you can explore shapes on 1-2-3-5 similarly. Below are a few possibilities. Get them making up their own.

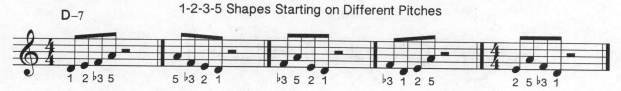

As with all of the shapes that we introduce, *your students need to visualize each shape coming out of a scale.* We have had success alternating between the first five notes of the scale (1-2-3-4-5) and the shape (1-2-3-5) in tempo. For example:

You can also descend the first five notes of the scale:

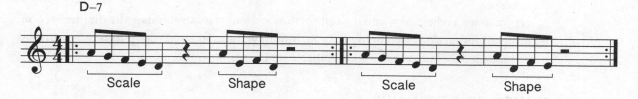

MOVING FROM CHORD TO CHORD

In jazz, improvisers need to create lines that move smoothly from one chord to another. The strongest way to do this is to point out the notes that change from one chord/scale to the next. In the case of D–7 moving to F–7, the most obvious note change is A (the 5th of D–7) moving to A♭ (the 3rd of F–7).

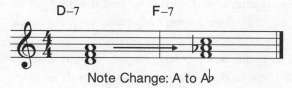

To highlight this half-step difference, make A the *last* note in D minor, and A♭ the *first* note in F minor. For example:

Accentuating half-step voice leading is important in every situation that uses more than one chord/scale. More on that later.

As a glimpse of where we are headed, when moving from one chord to another you can also point out what's *the same* between the two. For example, both D Dorian and F Dorian share the pitches G, C, and D. The usual term for this is using "common tones."

Common Tones (C, D, G) Shared by D–7 and F–7

Playing what's different from chord to chord makes a line harmonically strong, while playing common tones highlights the bass motion. Both approaches are necessary, but playing too many common tones can result in solos that are harmonically nondescript. They can also seem to have little forward motion.

THE METRONOME IN REHEARSAL

As a reminder, use a metronome clicking on 2 and 4 in rehearsal. Once your students are comfortable locking in with this, have it click on *only* 2 or *only* 4 (one click per measure). This way they have to take a more active part in creating a time feel rather than reacting to an external time-keeper.

If you have a rehearsal without a full rhythm section, you can simulate the rhythm section by using apps that do the comping for you. You might also use play-along recordings such as those produced by Jamey Aebersold, available on iTunes or Amazon.

TUNES TO BEGIN WITH

In starting to improvise, we recommend playing on a modal tune like Miles Davis's "So What," or John Coltrane's "Impressions" (both have the same chord progression). The Jamey Aebersold book, *Maiden Voyage*, also contains a set of tunes selected for beginning improvisers.

MORE ADVANCED RHYTHMS (3/4 + 2/4)

As your students develop, they may need help creating new rhythms (beyond the rhythms we introduced in chapter 2). When listening to jazz, they should always pay attention to rhythmic ideas to develop their own rhythmic sense.

Here is a more advanced curriculum for rhythmic development. As soon as your students are comfortable with syncopation, introduce them to rhythms that group the beats in interesting ways. We start by combining rhythms that imply 3/4 or 2/4.

ADDING THE 2ND (1-2-3-5)

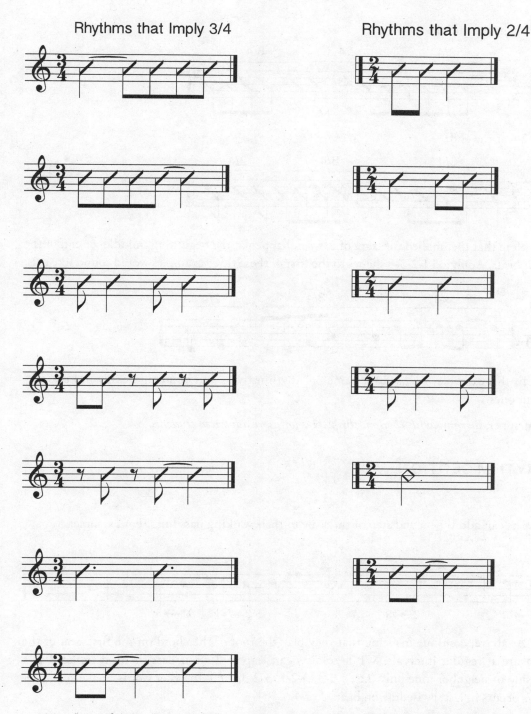

Two bars of 4/4 contain eight beats. We can group these eight beats into 3 beats, 3 beats, and 2 beats (two bars of 3/4 and one bar of 2/4). The examples below use the first rhythm from the 3/4 column and the fourth rhythm from the 2/4 column (above).

2/4 at the beginning:

2/4 in the middle:

2/4 at the end:

Note that the implied measure of 2/4 can happen at the beginning, middle, or end of the eight beats. Applying 1-2-3-5 shapes to the first of these three examples would sound like this:

In this example, we used the same 3/4 rhythm twice, but you could easily use two different ones.

Remember, *working with rhythms this way is for more advanced students.*

RHYTHM SECTION

Bass

Bassists can add the second step of the scale to their walking bass lines. For example:

As above, continue insisting that they play the root of the chord on the first beat of the measure at regular intervals. While soloists can leap to 2, your bassists need to use 2 as a passing or neighbor tone only (i.e., 1-2-3, 3-2-1, 3-2-3, etc.). In other words, make sure 2 always occurs in a stepwise line on beats 2 or 4.

CHAPTER 4

APPROACHING CHORD TONES FROM BELOW

In the previous chapter we added the 2nd step of the scale to the triad. In this chapter, we add notes we call "approach tones." They are a half-step below each note of the triad and serve to make melodies more interesting.

Two of these approach tones, a half-step below the root and a half-step below the 5th, don't belong to the chord/scale. For now, each approach tone must immediately move to a chord tone (see below).

Reminder: Unless stated otherwise, teach each step of every lesson plan by call and response. You sing and/or play; they sing and/or play.

Lesson Plan 5: Approach Tones (Half-Step Below)

RECOMMENDED RECORDING, LESSON PLAN 3: SONNY ROLLINS, *SAXOPHONE COLOSSUS*. Recommended track: "Saint Thomas."

1. Have the students sing and play the following scale study together.

Have your students repeat this pattern on F Dorian and two or three other scales from the repertoire you are working on. This will ensure that chapter 8 won't feel overwhelming when you get there. If you don't have specific repertoire you're working on, see the Teacher's Notes at the end of chapter 2 for a recommended sequence of chords to add to your practice.

2. Have your class sing and play the following exercise together. At first, have them sing and play these pitches rubato with the rhythm section sustaining the chord. Then have them sing it and play it a few more times, but in tempo.

(In the example , "AT" = <u>A</u>pproach <u>T</u>one.)

Point out to your students that they are simply approaching the pitches of the root triad by a half-step. Play slowly enough that they hear (and feel) that two of the approach tones don't fit the scale.

3. Sing and play several triad shapes together. After each one, sing and play it again with half-step below approach tones. Use the rhythms in the following examples:

4. Help your students make up their own triad shapes (one student gives the first note, someone else the second, etc.). Play the shape by itself; then play it with half-step below approach tones (as above). Alternate singing and playing.

   Stick exclusively to the rhythms demonstrated in the examples above. Make up as many shapes as possible so the class will get used to adding approach tones to any note-order and contour.

5. As a class, sing and play this group of eight pitches in order. *Repeat until memorized.*

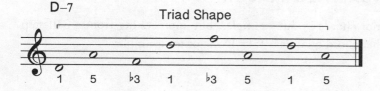

6. Using the eight-note shape from step 5 (above), have each student improvise rhythms and choose whether to use approach tones. If they wish, they can repeat some notes. For example:

   If eight notes are too many, start with two or three. As always, feel free to adjust each step to fit your students' skill level.

7. Repeat steps 3 through 7 on F minor and one or two other chords from the repertoire you are performing.

Teacher's Notes

UPBEATS AND ANTICIPATION

The rhythms in this chapter are a key component of jazz language. Just as downbeats are the most important rhythmic placements in classical music, upbeats are the most important in jazz. For a jazz musician, the upbeat of four (often called the "and" of four) is more important than the downbeat of beat one. Starting and ending phrases with upbeats creates forward motion rhythmically and melodically. This sets the stage for more rhythmic soloing and for playing chords just before they arrive (something jazz musicians call "anticipation"). Training your students to play chord tones early (an 8th-note before the beat as in this chapter) is a great introduction to this motto: *if you're not early, you're late*. If this doesn't make sense to you right now, don't worry . . . it will by the end of the book.

Rhythms naturally drive melodic content. We've designed this curriculum so that your students play rhythms that give them an intuitive understanding of jazz language. For example, this chapter doesn't use the seven rhythms from chapter 2 because those rhythms are less effective with approach tones. Over time, the rhythms your students practice will come together, as will the types of melodic lines they express.

DIFFERENT CHORD QUALITIES (MAJOR)

So far, we have only used minor chords in our examples, but approaching from a half-step below is just as effective on other chord qualities. Take D major for example:

RHYTHM SECTION

Drums: Lightly Kicking Upbeats

If your drummer is feeling comfortable locking in the ride cymbal and hi-hat with the bass, they may *lightly* play the rhythms from this chapter with the left hand (snare) and bass drum. As always, these things need to be done *without impacting the time/feel of the ride cymbal pattern*. This requires an ever-increasing amount of coordination and independence.

While your class works on step 4 of the lesson plan from this chapter, you might have your drummer lightly kick the band on the "and" of two and "and" of four by pairing a drum with a light cymbal crash. As the great Al Foster was fond of saying, it can be useful to think of the snare drum as a trumpet section, and the bass drum as a trombone section, and use those drums the way you would write an arrangement using trumpets and trombones.

Piano/Guitar: Approaching 3, 7 | 5, 9 Voicings from Below

If your pianist is more advanced, teach them that they can approach chord tones from a half-step below as well. For example:

APPROACHING CHORD TONES FROM BELOW

3, 7 | 5, 9 Voicings

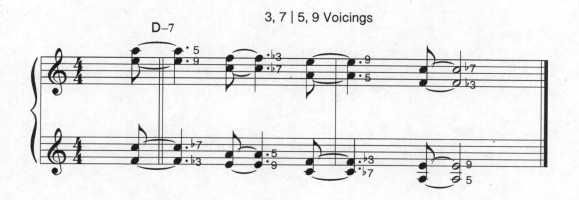

Approaching 3, 7 | 5, 9 Voicings from a Half-Step Below

This method of using approach tones works with all of the voicing options discussed in chapter 2. This is also true of the guitar and is particularly simple because students can just start a shape one fret lower and slide it up to the chord in order to approach the chord tones from below.

CHAPTER 5

APPROACHING CHORD TONES FROM ABOVE

In the last chapter, we approached the pitches in the root triad by a half-step from below. In this chapter, we approach the root triad by a scale-step from above.

Lesson Plan 6: Approaching Chord Tones from a Scale Step Above

RECOMMENDED RECORDING, LESSON PLAN 6: HANK MOBLEY, *ROLL CALL*. Recommended track: "My Groove, Your Move."

1. Have your students sing and play the following scale study together.

Follow this study with the one at the beginning of chapter 4. Sing and play also. Here it is again for reference:

Repeat these patterns on other chord/scales as well. As we move forward, going over previous scale studies needs to be a part of your daily routine. This will be key to your students' understanding and success with chapter 8.

2. Approach the root triad by scale-step from above.

As before, have your students play and sing this rubato, with the rhythm section sustaining the chord. Play slowly enough that your students hear (and feel) that the approach tone is slightly more dissonant than the notes of the triad when played with the sustained chord in the rhythm section, and that moving to a pitch from the root triad resolves the dissonance. When ready, play it in time.

3. Sing and play several triad shapes together. Collaborate (one student gives the first note, someone else the second, etc.). With each new shape, sing and play it a second time, approaching each chord tone by a scale-step above. Use the rhythms in the following examples:

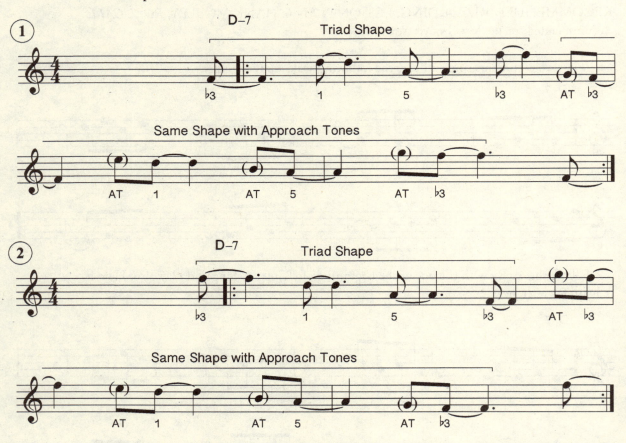

If a four-note triad shape (as above) is too complicated for your students to use approach tones, start with two- or three-note shapes.

4. As in Lesson Plan 5 (chapter 4), sing and play this group of eight pitches in order. *Repeat until memorized.*

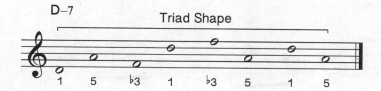

5. Using the eight-note shape from step 4 (above), have each student improvise rhythms and choose whether to use approach tones. Some of the pitches can be repeated (see measure 3). For example:

If eight notes are too many, start with two or three. As always, feel free to adjust each step to fit your students' skill level.

8. Repeat steps 3 through 7 on F minor and with one or two other chords from your repertoire.

Lesson Plan 7: 8th-Note Lines with Approach Tones

RECOMMENDED RECORDING, LESSON PLAN 7: HANK MOBLEY, *ROLL CALL*.
Recommended track: "Roll Call."

1. Just as in Lesson Plan 6, have the class sing and play the following scale studies together.

Repeat these patterns on F minor and other chord/scales found in your repertoire. Remember, going over previous scale studies needs to be a part of your daily routine. Chapter 8 is looming in the distance.

2. Play a five-note triad shape below or create your own.

This example is easy but play it at a very slow tempo. We're going to gradually add things to it which make it much more complicated.

3. One by one, approach each pitch from a scale-step above, like this:

And so on, until every triad pitch has an approach tone from above. When you have added approach tones to every pitch in the five-note triad shape, it will sound like this:

Before adding more approach tones, make sure your students can easily play the above examples at the tempo you have chosen.

You can see how difficult this line *could* be if played quickly. By playing it slowly until every note feels comfortable, you lay the groundwork for speeding it up.

4. Notice that the end of the line lands on a downbeat. This could be made more interesting by adding one extra note at the end of the line like this:

The extra note creates syncopation and adds rhythmic interest and forward momentum. Your students have a basic choice to make at the end of every melodic line: play a downbeat or an upbeat. Some lines should end on downbeats, and others not. Keep endings unpredictable.

5. Follow the process in steps 3 and 4 to approach your triad shape from a half-step *below*. It will eventually sound like this:

Your students will now have the option of using one approach tone or the other: scale-step above or half-step below.

6. Practice randomizing which approach tone you choose. For example:

When your students are ready, apply this process to a few other chords found in your repertoire.

Teacher's Notes

RHYTHM SECTION

Bass: Adding Approach Tones to Bass Lines

Bassists can also use approach tones to design bass lines. Have them play triad pitches on beats 1 and 3 and approach tones on beats 2 and 4. Once they're comfortable with quarter notes, they can occasionally play the upbeat of four, as we did in the lesson plans in this chapter:

Piano

Pianists, if advanced enough, can approach the chord tones in their voicings from a scale-step above.

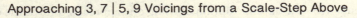

Approaching 3, 7 | 5, 9 Voicings from a Scale-Step Above

CHAPTER 6

APPROACHING CHORD TONES BY TWO NOTES

Once your students are comfortable approaching chord tones by one note, they are ready to introduce multiple approach tones. This may take a little bit to get used to, but it's not any more difficult to hear than single note approaches.

Lesson Plan 8: Two-Note Approach Tones (Above/Below)

RECOMMENDED RECORDING, LESSON PLAN 8: WAYNE SHORTER, *SPEAK NO EVIL*. Recommended track: "Speak No Evil."

1. Have your students sing and play the following scale study together:

As you can see, this study is nothing more than diatonic thirds, alternating direction (one third goes up, the next goes down). Repeat this pattern on other chord/scales.

When you review the previous scale studies in your daily routine, you might change up the rhythm like this:

This will get your students ready for chapter 8. Although the rhythmic change is simple, the effects on your students' playing will be far-reaching. We promise.

2. Have your students sing and play the following two-note approach together:

Root Triad with Two Approaches (Above and Below)

Notice that we're combining the approach tones from the previous lesson plans (scale-step above with the half-step below). As with other lesson plans, have your students play and sing the above example rubato with the rhythm section sustaining the chord. If your students sing this once or twice, it will help cement the sound in their ears.

3. As before, create a few different triad shapes and apply this two-note approach (above-below) to those shapes. Use the following rhythm to play the shapes you create in time:

If four-note triad shapes (as in the example above) are too complicated, begin with two- or three-note shapes. In a short time, your students will be ready for four-note shapes.

4. Repeat steps 2 and 3 on F minor and other chords from your repertoire.
5. Improvise triad shapes, alternating between the shape by itself, and the shape with this two-note approach (above-below). Allow your students to experiment with rhythm a bit but help them include the rhythm from step 3 as well. For example:

APPROACHING CHORD TONES BY TWO NOTES

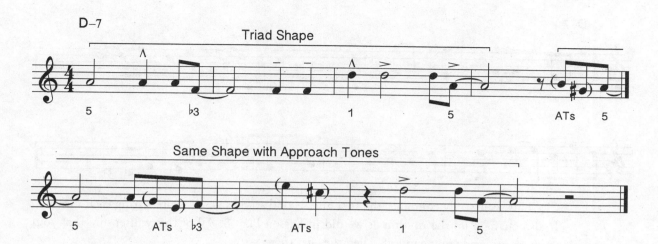

Lesson Plan 9: Approaching Chord Tones from Two Notes Above or Two Notes Below

RECOMMENDED RECORDING, LESSON PLAN 9: MILES DAVIS SEXTET, *1958*. Recommended track: "Love for Sale."

The same process we used with the above-below approach in Lesson Plan 8 works with all two-note approaches.

1. Have your students sing and play the following scale study together.

Repeat this pattern on F minor and other chord/scales from your repertoire.

Keep reviewing previous scale studies in your daily routine. The following is an example of one way to do this:

This scale study combines the first and second studies we did, alternating each measure. It also changes up the rhythm as we did in Lesson Plan 8. All of this will ensure that your students are ready for chapter 8 when they get there.

2. Sing and play a two-note approach that uses two half-steps above *or* two half-steps below the chord tone.

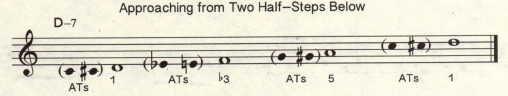

As before, sing and play this rubato with the rhythm section sustaining the chord.

This seems like an appropriate time to repeat something we said earlier: Slow, steady tempos allow the body and mind to coordinate themselves with greater ease. There's a fine teacher by the name of Ignatius Kendell who is fond of saying, "Fast is nothing more than slow, faster."

When your students are ready, use the same rhythms from Lesson Plan 8 to play these two-note approaches. Here's an example approaching from two half-steps above:

3. Create a few triad shapes and apply two-note approaches to them. As before, have the class collaborate. We recommend approaching the chord tones from two half-steps above.

When using these two-note approaches, you must approach the 3rd of a minor chord and the 3rd of a major chord differently. In major chords, approach the 3rd from below; in minor chords, approach the 3rd from above. For example:

Approaching the 3rd of a major triad from below:

Approaching the 3rd of a minor triad from above:

4. Repeat steps 2 and 3 on F minor and other chords from your repertoire.
5. Have your students improvise triad shapes, alternating between the shape by itself, and the shape with this two-note approach.

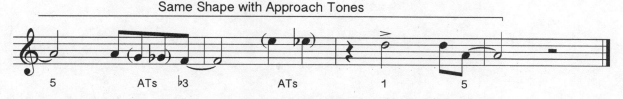

A student capable of improvising something like the above is much further along than usual. Some, of course, won't be familiar enough with the materials to do this right now. But it is possible. Don't be surprised if this step feels like a roadblock to some of your students for a minute. You can always simplify the task by limiting the number of notes in the triad and pre-deciding a couple of rhythms to play. Make no mistake, this is actually pretty good.... If we had a younger student do that, we'd be reasonably excited about their future.

CHAPTER 7

APPROACHING CHORD TONES BY THREE OR MORE NOTES

In this chapter your students will practice approaching chord tones with three or more notes. They will also begin improvising on the 7th-chord built from the root. Following this chapter, your students will be ready to move beyond triad-based melodies.

Reminder: Unless stated otherwise, teach each step of every lesson plan by call and response. You sing and/or play; they sing and/or play.

Lesson Plan 10: Approaching with Three Notes (Part 1)

RECOMMENDED RECORDING, LESSON PLAN 10: MILES DAVIS, *COOKIN'*. Recommended track: "Oleo."

1. Have the class sing and play the following scale study together.

Repeat this pattern on F minor and other chord/scales from your repertoire.

Review previous scale studies in your daily routine. By now, your students will likely be ready to play eight consecutive 8th-notes using the patterns they have learned. For example:

As before, this will help your students be ready for chapter 8. This should concern you even more right now, because chapter 8 is next. Right next door. Waiting . . .

2. Have your students sing and play the following three-note approach.

Have the rhythm section proceed as always (sustain the chord).

3. Have your students create triad shapes and add these three-note approaches to them. At first, sing and play the three approaches as quarter notes. Below, we're using an extremely simple triad shape for ease of understanding. Your students should gradually create more complex triad shapes.

When that's comfortable, change the rhythm as follows:

Have the rhythm section assume their comping roles while the other students play the three-note approaches above.

4. Sing and play in 4/4 time, first playing the triad shape, then approaching the triad notes with three 8th-notes (below-above-below). Be sure to place the chord tones *on* the beat:

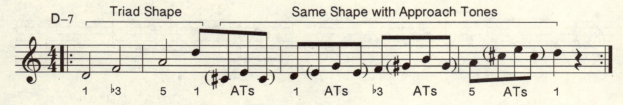

If this is too difficult for your students, see the Teacher's Notes at the end of the chapter for ideas on how to simplify this step.

5. As in previous lesson plans, improvise on triad shapes, alternating between the shape by itself, and the shape with three-note approaches. Let your students know that they don't have to use approach tones on every triad pitch (see the last line of the example below):

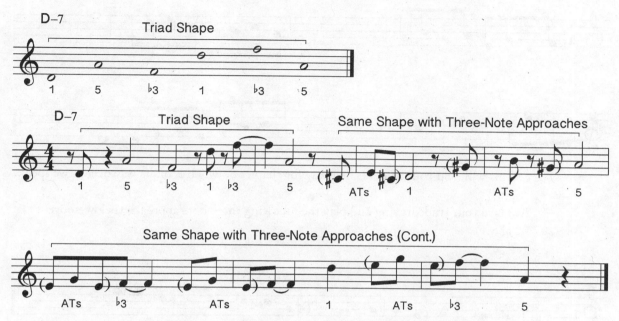

As you can see, the D and the A near the end of the above example do not have approach tones. When several pitches have approach tones, it's important to use the occasional triad pitch *without* approaches. This keeps the line less predictable, and, therefore, more interesting.

Lesson Plan 11: Approaching with Three Notes (Part 2)

RECOMMENDED RECORDING, LESSON PLAN 11: MILES DAVIS, *RELAXIN'*. Recommended track: "If I Were a Bell."

1. Have the class sing and play the following scale study together:

Repeat this pattern on other chord/scales.

Review previous scale studies in your daily routine. As we said, your students will likely be ready to play eight consecutive 8th-notes using the patterns they have learned. For example:

This will help your students be ready for chapter 8, which is on its way over as we speak.

2. Have your students sing and play the following three-note approach (below-above-above).

3. Have the class create several triad shapes and add these three-note approaches to them. At first, have them play the three approach tones as quarter notes, just like they did in Lesson Plan 10.

Once that's comfortable, change up the rhythm as follows:

APPROACHING CHORD TONES BY THREE OR MORE NOTES

4. Have your students sing and play in 4/4 time, first playing the triad shape, then approaching each triad pitch with three 8th-notes (below-above-above). Be sure to place the chord tones *on* the beat.

As a reminder, we discuss simplifying this step in the Teacher's Notes at the end of the chapter.

5. Teach your students that, with these approaches, the 3rd of the major triad needs to be approached differently. On a major 3rd the approach must be inverted to become half-step above and two half-steps below. For example:

6. Improvise on triad shapes, alternating between the shape by itself, and the shape with approach tones. By design, we have used the same eight-note shape in several lesson plans. Your students need to experience how different a line can feel with each melodic device. Here's the eight-note shape again, this time over a major chord:

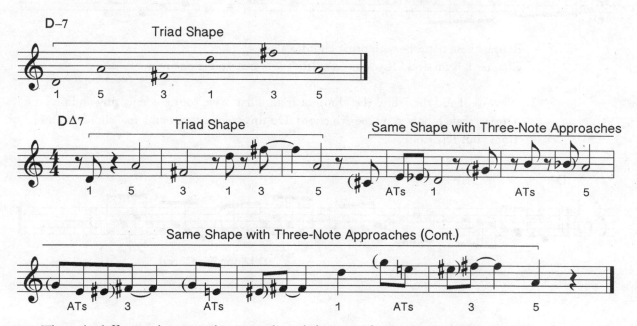

The only difference between this example and the example in Lesson Plan 10 (step 5) is the quality of the chord and the type of approach used.

Lesson Plan 12: Approaching the 7th

RECOMMENDED RECORDING, LESSON PLAN 12: DEXTER GORDON, *DOIN' ALLRIGHT*. Recommended Track: "It's You or No One."

1. Have your students sing and play the following scale studies together. They are the same as in Lesson Plan 11.

Repeat these patterns with other chord/scales.
Chapter 8 is on deck! If you need a drink of water, go get one now.

2. Now we'll add the 7th to the D minor triad. First, have your students sing and play a Dorian scale followed by the 7th chord. Do this several times on a few chords/scales from your repertoire.

APPROACHING CHORD TONES BY THREE OR MORE NOTES   59

3. Create 7th-chord shapes. Have your students sing and play them together, just as we did with triad shapes in previous lesson plans (i.e., rubato with rhythm section sustaining the chord). For example:

4. Add the following three-note approaches.

Note: Minor 7ths are approached the same way as minor 3rds (half-step below, two-steps above).

Similarly, *major 7ths are approached the same way as major 3rds (scale-step above, two-steps below).*

5. Let your students improvise, choosing a 7th chord shape that they ornament with three-note approaches. At first, use the following rhythm:

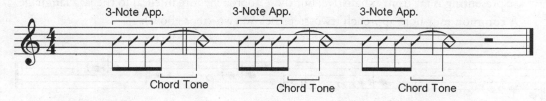

For example:

Once that rhythm feels comfortable on a few chords/scales, use the following rhythm:

For example:

Teacher's Notes

APPROACHING WITH FOUR OR FIVE NOTES

There are two more common approaches we want to introduce: a four- and a five-note approach. You may decide not to work on these at this point—it's up to you. The next chapter deals with improvising on the entire chord/scale, and your students may well be tired of dealing with triad-based melodies. Still, we want to show you these options to encourage your students to get creative with approach tones and prepare them for a later chapter. Again, what we are presenting is far from exhaustive, but these approaches are integral to the jazz language.

A common four-note approach (two-steps below, two-steps above):

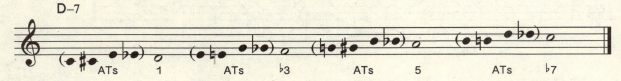

A common five-note approach (two below, two above, half-step below):

Another common four-note approach (four half-steps above):

Note that, on a minor chord, we can approach the minor 3rd and minor 7th from above in this manner. On a major chord, however, this approach works best going to the root or the 5th. *Basically, whenever there's a major 3rd between two chord tones, you can fill it in with a chromatic scale, up or down.*

You can repeat the steps from previous lesson plans to teach these approaches to your students (i.e., design your own 7th chord shapes, create a rhythm that ensures that the chord tone falls on the "and" of 4 OR 1, and then ornament the shape with approach tones).

SIMPLIFYING THREE-NOTE APPROACHES FOR LESS EXPERIENCED STUDENTS

If approaching an entire triad shape with three notes feels overwhelming to your students, try this exercise, which approaches each chord tone, one at a time.

Once they are comfortable with that, you can begin to ornament two chord tones at a time:

Ornamenting one note at a time is effective with any of the approaches we've learned in chapters 4 through 7.

CHAPTER 8

IMPROVISING ON THE ENTIRE CHORD/SCALE (PART 1)

In this chapter, we begin improvising with the entire chord/scale.

For these concepts to be effective, your students need experience with chapters 2–7. They need to *hear* the triad as the tonal center of gravity in the chord/scale, and by now, we think they can. If they cannot, more singing is the answer: sustain the root of the chord on the piano (or have your bassist sustain the root) while you play the scale, and they sing the root triad. A little bit of directed practice like this can make all the difference. As we said earlier, if your students don't aurally recognize the root triad as the tonal center of gravity, they will end up treating every note in the scale equally. This means that their improvising will tend to wander and be ambiguous.

Until now, every lesson plan has included scale studies. *If your students have not gained basic mastery of those studies, they **will not** be able to absorb the material presented in this chapter.*

Lesson Plan 13: Diatonic Thirds

RECOMMENDED RECORDING, LESSON PLAN 13: SONNY ROLLINS, *SONNY ROLLINS PLUS 4*. Recommended track: "Pent-Up House."

1. Tell your students, "From now on, we're going to improvise using all of the notes in a scale." Maybe have a small celebration.
2. Remind your students that they have been playing scales in thirds since Lesson Plan 3. For example:

Your students are now ready to think of these exercises differently: diatonic thirds that they can use any way they want. The structures they have practiced are melodically strong, so they can change up the order in any way they wish. For instance, they might swap the second and seventh measures in the above example. Or they might swap measures 2 and 3. If you play around with swapping measures, it should crack the door open in their minds so they begin to see that the sky's the limit.

3. The previous scale exercises have prepared your students to visualize the thirds within a scale in sets of two. Show them the following illustration:

Remind your students of the four shapes they have already practiced:

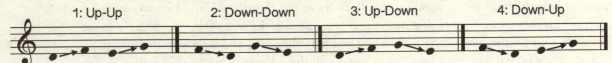

In the example above, the four options are applied to the first two thirds in a D Dorian scale (D/F, E/G). As always, practicing applying these to other scales as well.

4. Point out that they have applied each of these options to the full scale, going up and down. You might keep the "Pairs of Thirds" example visible (step 3 above) while they review each of these options. *Remember to sing and play.*

5. Practice each of the four options (i.e. up-up, down-down, up-down, down-up) on any of the chord/scales in your repertoire. Perhaps add a new scale that your students haven't yet learned.

   Remind your students that none of this is new; they have been doing this for several weeks.

6. Improvise on consecutive thirds, using the following rhythm:

   Have them move from one option to another *without being predictable*. It's helpful to repeat one option from time to time, but never more than twice in a row. For example:

7. One scale at a time, have your students improvise melodies (using pairs of thirds) that start high and wind up in the low register. Try not to let your students slip into thinking one third at a time.

   To reiterate, playing structures found in a scale (such as consecutive thirds) usually creates harmonically stronger lines with more interesting shapes. Keep in mind, descending melodies tend to be especially strong.

8. Let your students improvise using only consecutive thirds. Allow them the freedom to choose any rhythms they'd like. Make sure they keep the consecutive thirds intact (in our experience, students are quick to abandon thirds when they are asked to make up their own rhythms). Do this on one chord at a time (two if they are ready). For example:

For a more complete sequence of chords to practice, see the Teacher's Notes at the end of chapter 2.

Teacher's Notes

SINGING TETRACHORDS

To really have control over any scale, your students must be able to sing it. Singing is a window into their inner sense of hearing. Until they sing it, they don't really know what it sounds like; they don't *own* it. (What they hear in their mind is nothing more than *the idea* of the sound.)

One way to make singing scales easier is to break them into two parts called *tetrachords*. A tetrachord is four consecutive pitches, and there are five tetrachords that are most commonly used:

Tetrachords

These five tetrachords are the building blocks for most conventional chord/scales in jazz. Any seven- or eight-tone chord/scale can be built by combining two of these tetrachords. For example, a Dorian scale is two minor tetrachords separated by a whole step:

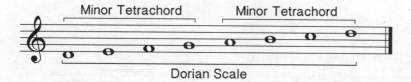

By the same token, a major scale is two major tetrachords separated by a whole step:

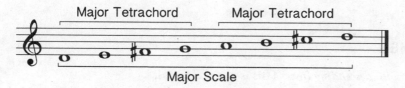

Your students don't need to be able to sing every single mode on the planet, they only need to be able to sing these five tetrachords. Then it's simply a question of combining them.

See the appendix in the back of the book for a more complete treatment of how tetrachords are used to construct chord/scales in jazz.

ADDING SYNCOPATION TO DIATONIC THIRDS

You can use thirds rhythmically by adding syncopation. Try inserting quarter- and 8th-rests every few beats. For example:

MORE ADVANCED USE OF THIRDS

When your students are ready, have them improvise 8th-note lines, ascending and descending, moving between each of the shapes unpredictably (with no recognizable pattern). For example:

DESCENDING LINES

We often begin scale work with descending lines. This is not accidental.

Descending lines are often less familiar to students. As teachers, we tend to start with the familiar, which risks under-emphasizing the less familiar. Also, playing a convincing descending melody is easier than playing a convincing ascending melody. It's kind of like following gravity: you get a strong beginning and ending almost by default.

RHYTHM SECTION

Bass: Using Diatonic Thirds in Bass Lines

Bassists can organize consecutive thirds in the same way. In straight-ahead jazz, as always, have them focus on quarter notes. For example:

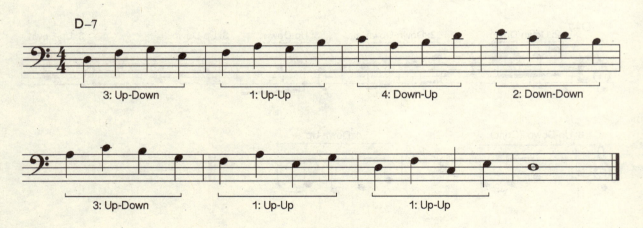

In bars 3 and 4, beat one is not a basic chord tone (1, 3, or 5). This is only acceptable because the chord being played lasts for more than four measures.

For music where chords change more frequently, guide your students towards the bass examples from previous chapters.

IMPROVISING ON THE ENTIRE CHORD/SCALE (PART 1) 69

Piano: Using Diatonic Thirds in Comping

Pianists can also use thirds in their comping. For example:

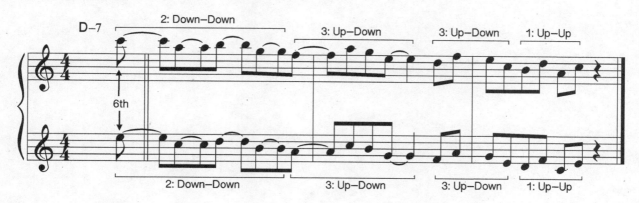

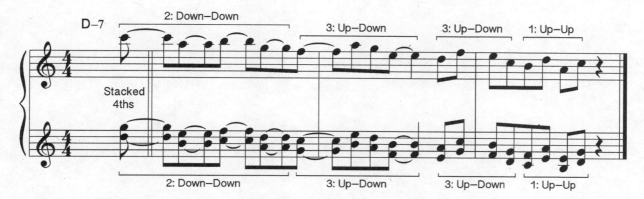

In this example we chose a single interval (such as a sixth or a fourth) and kept it intact while creating melodies built on thirds.

Note: If a soloist's lines are busy, this would not be appropriate (like we said before, if you hear two people talking at once, you can only focus on one at a time). Things like this should be played during rests or sustained notes.

As we mentioned in chapter 2, one particularly common voicing used by pianists and guitarists is a four-note voicing built by stacking two fourths and a third within the chord/scale:

Have your pianist be able to do this in every key, and your guitarist able to do this everywhere possible on the neck.

CHAPTER 9

IMPROVISING ON THE ENTIRE CHORD/SCALE (PART 2)

Longer Lines and Harmonic Changes

This chapter addresses two goals: creating longer lines with 3rds, and connecting lines that move between different chord/scales.

Lesson Plan 14: Creating Longer Lines with 3rds

RECOMMENDED RECORDING, LESSON PLAN 14: SONNY ROLLINS, *A NIGHT AT THE VILLAGE VANGUARD*. Recommended track: "Sonnymoon for Two."

1. Introduce your students to the following rhythm. Using the four options from chapter 8, have them design a melody out of thirds and apply it to the rhythm. For example:

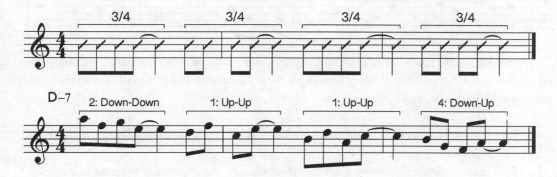

The result is a feeling of 3/4 played *against* the 4/4 meter.

Remember, the goal is to move from one option to another *without being predictable*. Point out how important it is to repeat choices from time to time. Never repeat a choice more than twice in a row (to make sure they don't fall into using the same pattern again and again).

2. Take out the first quarter note (E) in the rhythm from step 1. Do the same with the third quarter note (C). For example:

The resulting rhythm creates a feeling of 5/4 happening *against* the 4/4 meter.

3. Play the full line as a stream of 8th-notes.

If your students are having trouble with this step, simplify it by playing one measure at a time, or adding one note at a time to the line that you're playing. For example:

Note: You might point out to your students that, musically speaking, the most compelling line results from step 2 above (the rhythms that imply 5/4). The stream of 8th-notes has too much consistency to be rhythmically surprising.

4. Have your students create a few more melodies built from thirds, applying the rhythms of steps 2–3.
5. Have your students improvise with thirds on each of the rhythms presented (see steps 2, 3 and 4).

*Note: We say **improvise**. On this step, that means the sequence of thirds is up to them (they should mix them up). Remind them to play a different line with each step.*

Lesson Plan 15: Moving from One Chord/Scale to Another

RECOMMENDED RECORDING, LESSON PLAN 15: HANK MOBLEY, *SOUL STATION*. Recommended track: "This I Dig of You."

In this lesson plan, your students will improve their ability to visualize more than one chord/scale, side by side.

1. Choose two or three chord/scales from your repertoire. Write out each scale on the board, starting on the root (no need to label each pitch for your students as we have below; that's for your reference):

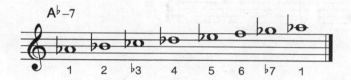

Check to see if any of the roots (in this case, D, F, and A♭) are present in every scale you selected. For example, the illustration above has three scales, and it's easy to see that one of the roots—the F in F–7—is present in all three. As always, if you have B♭ and E♭ instruments in your class, you might write the transposed scales as well.

Now, rewrite each scale starting from that common tone (F):

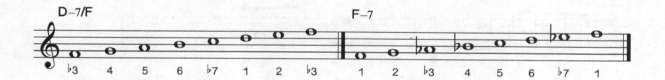

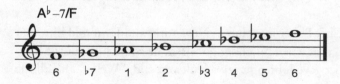

When you rewrite the scales in this way, your students can quickly see which notes stay the same and which notes change by half-step from one chord/scale to the next.

*Note: If the scales you selected do not have a root tone in common, rewrite each scale **starting as close to the same note as possible**.*

2. Play up AND down the first four notes of each chord/scale, starting each one as near to the same pitch as possible. Focus on seeing all the notes in one's mind (visualizing). Alternate between singing and playing.

As always, have the rhythm section sustain the chords if playing rubato, and comp if playing in tempo.

As your students are ready, add more notes to the scale. For example, they could play the first six notes of each scale, starting on the same pitch:

Or, the complete scale:

As we said before, alternating between singing and playing is critical. It will eventually demonstrate to the subconscious that *singing and playing are the same thing*. A quick story to illustrate this point.

John McNeil was talking with Chet Baker in a club in New York, and John told him that he wished he could sing like Chet, so that when his chops got tired, he could just put the horn aside and perform with his voice. Chet gave John a puzzled look and said, "Well . . . it's all the same thing, man."

3. Starting on the *root* of the first chord, play up one scale and down the next one. Notice that every scale change moves by step.

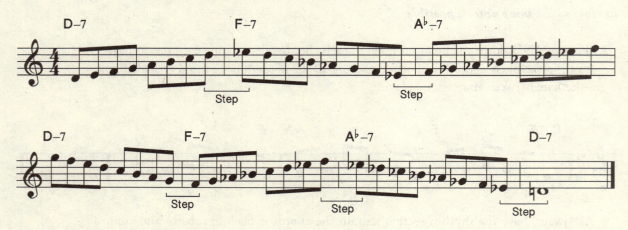

Again, our goal is to visualize the scales—to be able to picture all seven notes in one's mind, all at once. Your students will likely want to skip singing. Don't do it.

4. Play a descending line based on *one* of the four options your students have already learned. As always, the last note of one chord/scale needs to move by step to the next chord/scale. For example:

When your students are ready, have them combine *two* of the four options. Below is an example made of down-down and down-up.

As before, the above melody *moves by step* from one chord/scale to the other. Also, you may have noticed that all the examples in this lesson plan are descending. As a reminder, you need to practice ascending lines as well.

If it's too difficult for your students to play a line of 8th-notes over changing chords, have them use the practice rhythms from Lesson Plans 13 and 14 instead. To keep you from having to go searching, here they are as a reminder:

Practice Rhythm 1:

Practice Rhythm 2:

5. Choosing between the four basic shapes, improvise a descending line of thirds that moves by step through two or more chord/scales, using the following rhythm.

For example:

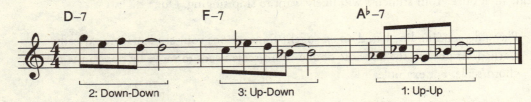

It may be helpful to write the scales on the board as we did before in order to help them visualize each chord/scale while they're improvising. Here they are again:

To help our students visualize the scales on their own, we have had success gradually erasing notes from the board as they play. If you have B♭ and E♭ instruments in your class, you might write the transposed scales as well.

6. Allow your students to improvise their own rhythms using pairs of thirds. Remember, always practice moving by step from one chord/scale to another. For example:

Note: The E♭ in measure one belongs to the F–7 chord in measure two. **Anticipating** *the chord in this way (playing it just before it arrives) gives this line the feeling of moving forward. As we said before, "If you're not early, you're late."*

CHAPTER 10

GENERAL SCALE SKILLS

Triads, 7th Chords, and Other Intervals

This chapter will show you how to apply the same process that we have learned with diatonic thirds to other structures in the chord/scale, including triads, 7th chords, 4ths, and other intervals.

Lesson Plan 16: Triads and Other Structures

RECOMMENDED RECORDING, LESSON PLAN 16: JOHN COLTRANE, *BLUE TRAIN*. Recommended track: "Moment's Notice."

1. Teach your students that they can build a triad on each step of the scale, just as they did with thirds. Imagine the triads in sets of two:

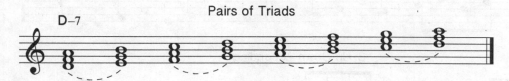

We want the students to think of each pair as a single sound. Help them avoid thinking of one triad at a time. You could eventually have them think of three or even four triads at once, as a set. They won't be able to play any of this quickly until they can see all of it at the same time, as a single idea.

2. As with thirds, apply the same four melodic options to the triads. As always, alternate singing and playing.

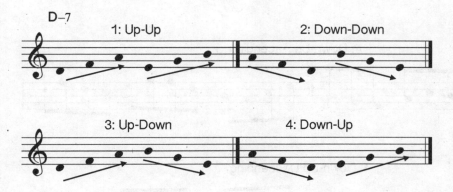

The Classroom Guide to Jazz Improvisation. John McNeil and Ryan Nielsen, Oxford University Press. © Oxford University Press 2024.
DOI: 10.1093/oso/9780197614648.003.0010

3. Apply each of these options to the full scale, whether going up or down the scale. Alternate singing and playing each of the following four options:

4. Have the class sing and play each of the four options (i.e., up-up, down-down, up-down, down-up) on all the scales they have used so far. Add more Dorian scales until the class can do these scale patterns on all twelve.
5. Have your students improvise, using the four options while playing the following rhythm:

They can fit two triads to this rhythm, and it should sound something like this:

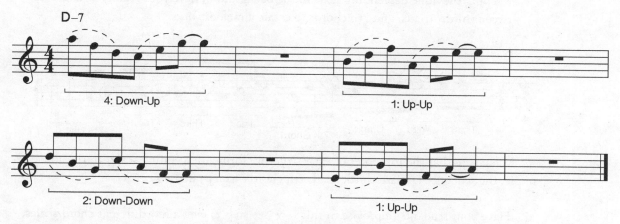

We recommend beginning with descending phrases. Adjust range to fit the needs of your students but be sure to keep the triad sets intact. Don't let them slip into thinking one triad at a time.

Start as high as you'd like and go down as low as you want.

Lesson Plan 17: Mixing It Up

RECOMMENDED RECORDING, LESSON PLAN 17: SHIRLEY SCOTT, *SOUL SHOUTIN'*. Recommended track: "Soul Shoutin'."

This lesson shows you how to combine thirds, triads, and 7th chords into one melodic line. We haven't yet had an entire lesson plan dealing with diatonic 7th chords, but they should feel accessible. After all, a 7th chord is just a triad with one extra third stacked on top.

1. Sing and play the following. Show your students that, in the example below, the top note of each triad forms a descending scale in the background:

The Descending Line
(The Top Note of Each Triad)

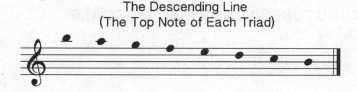

Split your class in half. Have one half sing the triads while the other half sings only the descending top-note line.

This line is particularly strong because of the descending scale in the background. Have your students memorize the pattern (from above): down-up, down-down, up-up, up-down. Sing and play it in at least a few keys. If range is a problem, start on a lower note in the scale and follow the same pattern.

If they can sing it, they hear it. And if they hear it, it will eventually show up in their playing.

2. Keeping the same descending scale in the background, have your students choose between thirds, triads, and 7th chords to create a melodic line.

Make sure that the top notes of each structure form a descending scale. In the above example, the sequence—triad, third, triad, 7th chord—is repeated twice.

3. Have your students improvise in this way (see step 2) over a few different chord/scales, one at time. Be sure they use all three structures (thirds, triads, and 7th chords).

Until now, they've only used one structure at a time, so this might be a bit of a leap. Choose a tempo that will let them have some success. Then point out that they are just starting with a descending scale and hanging something below each scale pitch.

4. Have your students improvise, combining all three structures, moving between a few chord/scales from your repertoire. *The top notes of the structures must form a descending stepwise line.* For example:

If you look at the top notes of each structure, you can see that the line in the background is A, G, F, E♭, D♭, D♭, C♭, and B♭. The last note of the second measure (the D♭) *anticipates* the A♭–7 chord by an 8th-note. This is another small illustration of our axiom, "If you're not early, you're late."

Teacher's Notes

ORGANIZING OTHER STRUCTURES IN THE CHORD/SCALE (7TH-CHORDS, INTERVALS)

You can follow the same steps using any structure. Just build it on each note of the scale. For example, with 7th chords:

1) Visualize them in sets of two:

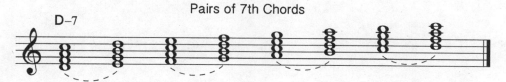

2) Apply the same four options as before:

This works just as well with other intervals, such as fourths. Just picture them in pairs:

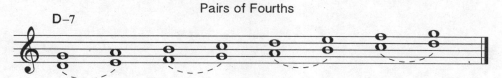

And apply the four basic options:

There's no limit to the structures you could imagine within a chord scale; *any shape from two to seven notes is fair game.* Whatever structures you discover or create together, imagine them in sets of two and apply the same four options.

COMBINING LESSONS

When reviewing previous lesson plans, place limits on what you ask your students to practice. Combining two concepts at a time (i.e., 1-2-3-5 + thirds) is more effective than saying, "Now use everything we've learned."

A good way to make a student (or even an excellent improviser) freeze up is to give them a half dozen options that must be included in their solo. Most of us can successfully hold two or three concepts in our mind at a time, but no more.

CHAPTER 11

UNDERSTANDING CHORD SYMBOLS AND RESPELLING CHORDS

If you are not fluent with chord symbols in jazz, it can be overwhelming to look at a chart full of them. Educators from around the United States have spoken with us about how daunting it is to decipher a chart with ten different chord qualities and be expected to teach their students how to improvise on them. We believe this chapter will simplify this.

First, Chord Symbols

Some explanations of chord symbols seem purposely dense and hard to understand. It would be much too cynical to say that the explainer wants to appear brilliant more than helpful, so we won't say that. But we will give you a strategy that makes your job easier.

Oftentimes, the confusion (understandably) comes from the chord symbols themselves, a natural result of the art form of jazz developing without any official way of doing things. The artists wrote what worked for them, and there were many ways to indicate that. For example, there are many symbols for C major. All an improviser would need is "C" or "Cmaj." But instead we see C∆9, C 6/9, C6, Cmaj13, CM7, and so on. Adding insult to injury, they all mean the same thing to the soloist—C major.

With that many chord symbols for major, imagine what a dominant 7th chord with a flatted 9th might look like. It's too horrible to put here. Unfortunately, you are going to run into this. Just for you, there's an appendix at the end of the book that has most of the chord symbols you will see and what they mean (in plain language). If you can't find them there, your music is either too hard or accidentally written backwards.

What Is Respelling?

Respelling is one way to simplify the written chord symbol. In this context, "respelling" means *mentally converting chords into a form that's easier to visualize.* It can also mean converting chords with different qualities into a progression where each chord quality is the same (see below). Respelling chords this way makes the changes between chord/scales much, much easier to see and use.

It turns out that, with few exceptions, most chord symbols belong to one of two families:

1) Dorian
2) Dorian with a raised 7th (ascending melodic minor)

Because of this, most chord/scales can be respelled as either a Dorian or minor/Δ7 scale. (By now, you're familiar with the first family of chords (Dorian). The second family—Dorian with a raised 7th—is also known as "minor/Δ7," simply notated as C– (Δ7).)

Let's look at a sample chord progression:

|| FΔ(♯11) | B7alt | G–7(♭5) | D7(♯11) | B♭Δ7(♯11) ||

That's a lot of chord qualities, and it's going to be tough for a student to visualize any kind of a line moving through them. But if you know how to respell them (and we will show you how), they become a series of manageable minor chords that move down by step. By respelling each chord, the original progression:

|| FΔ(♯11) | B7alt | G–7(♭5) | D7(♯11) | B♭Δ7(♯11) ||

becomes

|| D–7 | C– (Δ7) | B♭– (Δ7) | A– (Δ7) | G–7 ||

What appeared to be a complex chord progression with five different chord qualities becomes *a simple sequence of minor chords*. What does this mean for your students? If the *only* thing they know is the first five notes of their minor scales, they could see and hear something interesting (and easy to see) over this seemingly difficult progression:

In the above example, the written chord is above each measure; below is the respelling. The written pitches come from the first five steps of each respelling.

How to Respell

So how do you respell common chord qualities? We have a chart for you, using C as the root of each chord:

Chord Symbol	Its Minor Equivalent:	What That Means
CΔ7	Dorian built on the 6th	CΔ7 = A–7
C7	Dorian built on the 5th	C7 = G–7
C7alt	Minor/Δ7 built ½ step above root	C7alt = C♯– (Δ7)
C–7 (♭5) or ø	Minor/Δ7 built on the 3rd	Cø = E♭– (Δ7)

CHORD SYMBOLS AND RESPELLING CHORDS

Because we're not respelling anything that's already minor, *you only need to know four respellings to help your students:*

Two from the Dorian family:

- maj7 = Dorian built on the 6th
- V7 = Dorian built on the 5th

And two from the minor/Δ7 family:

- V7alt = minor/Δ7 built one half-step above the root
- min7 (♭5) [also known as half-diminished or ø] = minor/Δ7 built on the 3rd

Respelling does *not* change the harmony of a tune; it just helps students recognize patterns and relationships between chords (like common tones, common structures, voice-leading, etc.). This is not cheating; jazz musicians have done it for decades. (Professional jazz musicians use many additional respellings beyond the ones presented here.)

Whether your students can improvise on 1-2-3-5 shapes (chapter 3) or on the entire scale (chapters 8–10), respelling gives them a set of pitches that they can use effectively. They can think of respelling as an organizing tool. *It's a short cut to accessing the melodic structures they already hear*, no matter the chord quality or how experienced they are.

Note: Respelling is strictly for melodic consideration, and, therefore, should not be applied to the comping of the rhythm section (see the portion of this chapter marked "Rhythm Section" for more details).

The Teacher's Notes (at the end of the chapter) explain why these respellings work. You can also check out the appendix on Chord Symbols for more information.

Examples of Respelling

Here are some examples that respell common chord progressions in jazz. In each measure, we have included the 1-2-3-5 shape (chapter 3) of each minor respelling. *Again, the 1-2-3-5 shape represents the respelling, **not** the written chord symbol.*

Our first example resembles a chord progression from the jazz standard *Stella by Starlight* and the A sections of Dizzy Gillespie's "Woody 'n' You":

Above each measure you can see the written chord symbol; below each measure, the respelling of the chord. Playing this respelling results in stronger melodies and a progression that's easier to navigate.

Here's another example, similar to the tune "Solar":

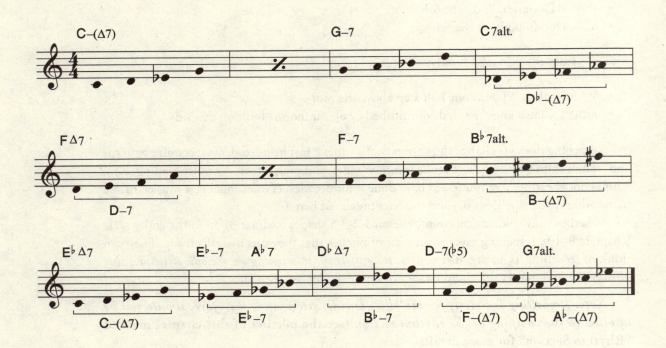

Respelling measure 10 allows your students to play the sound of E♭–7 throughout the measure. (Since your students aren't professional musicians, they might not be able to play both options in the last measure. We give our students the choice of doing one or the other: F–(Δ7) or A♭–(Δ7). While either of these will work, we feel that A♭–(Δ7) is a slightly stronger option.)

With the information from this chapter you can tackle most chord progressions, making chapters 2–10 immediately applicable to nearly every chord/scale. Study the table at the beginning of this chapter until its contents are clear to you. Here it is as a reminder:

Chord Symbol	Its Minor Equivalent:	What That Means
CΔ7	Dorian built on the 6th	CΔ7 = A–7
C7	Dorian built on the 5th	C7 = G–7
C7alt	Minor/Δ7 built ½ step above root	C7alt = C♯–(Δ7)
C–7(♭5) or ø	Minor/Δ7 built on the 3rd	Cø = E♭–(Δ7)

Extra Credit: Parallel Structures

> "It was a real revelation when I started seeing new parallel structures and different stepwise paths through the chord changes."
>
> —John McNeil

As we said before, one benefit of respelling is that you can see parallel structures between chords. For example, let's say you are playing a tune with the following chord progression:

|| G♭△7(♯11) | C–7 | A♭7alt ||

By respelling these chords with their minor equivalents, as taught in this chapter, the progression becomes:

|| E♭–7 | C–7 | A–(△7) ||

Where did we get these respellings?

- G♭△7 = E♭–7 (Dorian built on the 6th)
- C–7 stays the same
- A♭7alt = A– (△7) (minor/△7 one half-step above the root)

With this respelling, your students can move between three minor sounds rather than having to visualize a Lydian sound (G♭△), a minor sound (C–), and an altered sound (A♭7alt).

Let's take it one step further. As we learned in chapter 10, you can build triads on each step of a given scale. E♭ Dorian contains an F minor triad (the triad built on the 2nd step of the scale), C Dorian contains a G minor triad (the triad built on the 5th step of the scale); and the A– (△7) contains an A minor triad (the root triad).

The result: you can improvise over the original progression (G♭△7(♯11) | C–7 | A♭7alt) by outlining F– | G– | A–; three minor triads ascending by step:

This respelling implies ascending whole steps rather than the root motion played by the rhythm section. While the ideas themselves are simple (just triad pitches built on the respellings), the harmony they imply is fairly complex.

Respelling opens up a world of possibilities for an improviser; possibilities that are not readily apparent from the outset. It makes it easier for students to repeat ideas from one chord to the next, to see stepwise relationships between chord/scales, and generally results in much more interesting solos.

As you can imagine, there is a lot more to respelling than we could possibly explain within the scope of this text. For now, dealing with minor equivalents and looking for parallel structures between chord/scales (as in the respelling above) is a great place to begin.

Teacher's Notes

If you're curious about how we arrived at respelling each of the chords in this chapter with their minor equivalent, *this section is for you.*

RESPELLING THE DOMINANT

Let's start with a C7 chord. We respell C7 as a G–7 (minor built on the 5th). Consider how an F major scale contains the scales for both G–7 and C7. C7 is the 5th mode of F major (mixolydian) and G– is the 2nd mode (Dorian):

Every time you see a dominant chord symbol, think to yourself, "Minor built on the 5th."

RESPELLING THE ALTERED DOMINANT

Before explaining how we arrive at respelling an altered dominant, we should point out something. Describing the contents of an altered dominant scale to your class is one sure way to make them feel confused, intimidated, lost, bored, frightened or a number of other negative emotions. That said, here's a theoretical explanation for you, the teacher.

An altered scale contains the root, 3rd, and 7th of a dominant chord plus four altered pitches. Those four pitches are: ♭9, ♯9, ♯4, and ♯5. Below you can see the G altered scale and compare it with the A♭– (Δ7) scale starting from G. You can easily see that, enharmonically, they are identical.

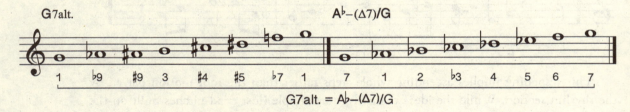

You can also see that the one on the left is very difficult to visualize. The one on the right is just a minor/(Δ7) scale starting from the major 7th.

If you, the teacher, are unfamiliar with these sounds, by all means sit at the piano and play the root, 3rd and 7th of a dominant in your left hand and move up and down the minor/Δ7 scale built a half-step above the root. Sing along with your right hand and experiment with moving up and down the scale melodically (perhaps singing something in 3rds).

Every time you see an altered dominant chord symbol, think to yourself, "Minor built one half-step above the root."

RESPELLING THE HALF-DIMINISHED CHORD

However it's labeled ("half-diminished," "min7(♭5)," or "ø") the minor/Δ7 respelling we use for this chord is built on the minor 3rd. For example:

As with the altered dominant, if you, the teacher, are unfamiliar with the half-diminished sound, play it at the piano; only this time, voice the root, ♭5 and ♭7 of the chord in your left hand, and with your right hand play the minor/Δ7 scale built on the 3rd. Sing along with your right hand, as you did with the altered dominant, singing short melodies within the sound of the chord/scale.

Every time you see a half-diminished chord symbol, think to yourself, "Minor/Δ7 built on the 3rd."

Important reminder: Even though we are talking a lot about the minor/Δ7 chord, in jazz the default minor is still Dorian!

RESPELLING LYDIAN

The tones of Lydian are the same as a Dorian scale built on the 6th:

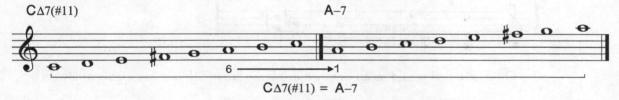

As you can see, CΔ7(♯11) is identical to the A–7 built on C.

Every time you see a Lydian chord symbol, think to yourself, "Minor built on the 6th."

RHYTHM SECTION

Respelling is strictly for melodic consideration.

When comping, *rhythm section players should choose sounds based on the written chord, NOT the respellings.* That said, here are a few notes on respelling for members of the rhythm section.

Bass: Only Respell When Soloing

Bassists still need to play the written roots of the chords, especially on the first beat of the measure. You'll need to be careful about teaching respelling to your bassist; it may tempt them away from their role of playing the actual written changes (chords). That way lies madness. Bassists should only use respellings when they are soloing, and *not any other time.*

Piano/Guitar: Voicing the Altered Dominant, When to Respell

Rather than thinking of respelling an *altered dominant,* at first your pianist/guitarist should simply alter the 5th and 9th within the 3-5-7-9 voicings they already know. To do this, raise or lower both the 5th and 9th by one half-step. For example:

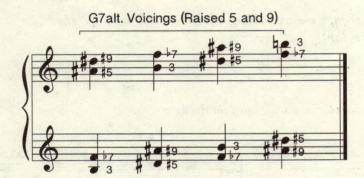

On guitar, that would mean simply moving the 5th or 9th one fret higher or lower:

The same is true of four-note voicings on the guitar:

CHORD SYMBOLS AND RESPELLING CHORDS   91

There is one chord where the comping instrument can respell for a more effective voicing: the *half-diminished* chord, or min7(♭5). For example, on a D–7(♭5) they can voice F– (Δ7):

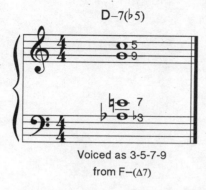

Voiced as 3-5-7-9
from F–(Δ7)

One last thing: if you have a II–7(♭5) | V7alt progression, respelling can be helpful for your pianist/guitarist. For example, the respelling for D–7(♭5) | G7alt is F– (Δ7) | A♭– (Δ7); two minor chords that are a minor 3rd apart:

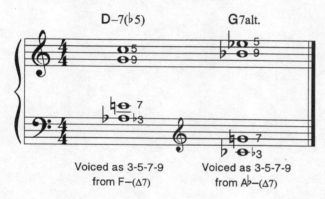

Voiced as 3-5-7-9   Voiced as 3-5-7-9
from F–(Δ7)   from A♭–(Δ7)

CHAPTER 12

THE II–7 | V7 | I∆7 (PART 1)

Using ♭7 to 3 to Move from Chord to Chord

The II–7 | V7 | I∆7 may be the most common chord progression in jazz. This chapter shows you how to create melodies that strongly define this sound.

Reminder (one more time, for good measure): Unless stated otherwise, teach each step of every lesson plan by call and response. You sing and/or play; they sing and/or play.

Lesson Plan 18: Hearing ♭7 to 3 Voice Leading on II–7 | V7 | I∆7

RECOMMENDED RECORDING, LESSON PLAN 18: ART FARMER AND GERRY MULLIGAN, *NEWS FROM BLUEPORT*. Recommended track: "Blueport."

To improvise on a II–7 | V7 | I∆7, your students need to learn what it sounds like. To this end, Lesson Plan 18 is designed for ear training, and doesn't have any steps involving choice or improvisation.

1. Write the following exercise in a few keys. Sing and play it in several keys, accompanied only by the bass playing whole-notes on the roots of each chord.

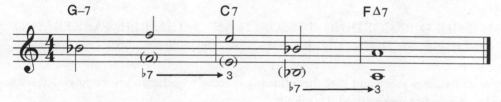

Your students can choose any octave for the 7th of each chord. *Whichever octave they choose, the 7th must move down a half-step to the 3rd of the next chord.* Point out that the 7th of one chord is like an approach tone to the 3rd of the next. Per usual, play this rubato at first with the rhythm section clearly sustaining each chord as you change from one chord to the next.

2. Add approach tones to the 3rd and 7th of each chord.

Play and sing this (rubato) while the rhythm section clearly sounds each chord.

The Classroom Guide to Jazz Improvisation. John McNeil and Ryan Nielsen, Oxford University Press. © Oxford University Press 2024.
DOI: 10.1093/oso/9780197614648.003.0012

3. Add the following rhythm to the melody:

Remind your students to play the ♭7 to 3 resolution in different octaves. It's a good way to maintain interest, and they get comfortable accessing different registers as they improvise.

4. Repeat steps 1, 2, and 3 in several keys. Apply them to any II–7 | V7 | IΔ7 found in your students' repertoire.

Teacher's Note

Lesson Plans 19, 20, and 21 are quite short. We anticipate students needing extra time with each of these steps.

These lesson plans require the ability to improvise using the materials from previous chapters, particularly chapters 2 and 3. If that foundation is not in place, your students will likely feel overwhelmed. A review may be needed.

We have had little success giving students an entire II–7 | V7 | IΔ7 progression at once. Instead, we have them practice II–7 going to V7, improvising on the II–7 chord only. Next, we repeat the process moving from V7 to IΔ7, improvising on the V7 chord only. With those pieces in place, they are much more likely to have success playing the entire II–7 V7 IΔ7.

Lesson Plan 19: Using ♭7 to 3 Voice Leading to Improvise on II–7 | V7

RECOMMENDED RECORDING, LESSON PLAN 19: CHARLIE PARKER AND DIZZY GILLESPIE, *BIRD AND DIZ*. Recommended track: "Bloomdido."

1. Have your students sing and play the following exercise together in several keys. Repeat until everyone has internalized the sound.

As always, your rhythm section should comp in tempo while the rest of the students play this.

2. Once comfortable with step 1 in several keys, have your students take turns improvising 1-2-3-5 shapes on G–7. Do this over the first three beats of the measure (now indicated by slashes below). Give each student a chance at this, moving through the whole class. (While one student is improvising, the rest of the class alternates singing and playing the last two notes of the first measure—in this case F to E.) Each soloists plays these

two bars twice, first singing, then playing. At the end, go through the whole class again, as slowly as needed. There should be no stopping; there should be some pressure to keep up.

Here are a few examples:

If you think that some students may feel overwhelmed by improvising like this, have the class play through the examples we've provided. That way, some of the students having trouble will experience success with these sounds. As always, teach by call and response.

3. Repeat steps 1 and 2 in at least six keys.

We recommend moving from key to key by descending whole steps. For example:

G–7 | C7
F–7 | B♭7
E♭–7 | A♭7
And so on.

Descending in whole-steps will get your students through six keys (if you descend whole-steps seven times, you end up back where you started). If you'd like to practice the other six keys, simply start the sequence a half-step higher. (For example, beginning with the key of C, you would move through the keys in the following order: C, B♭, A♭, F♯, E, D. *Then* E♭, D♭, B, A, G, F.) If your students have some trouble (say, with the key of D♭), remind them: there are no hard keys. There are only keys that they haven't played as much.

Lesson Plan 20: Using ♭7 to 3 Voice Leading to Improvise on V7 | IΔ7

RECOMMENDED RECORDING, LESSON PLAN 20: CHARLIE PARKER AND DIZZY GILLESPIE, *BIRD AND DIZ*. Recommended track: "An Oscar for Treadwell."

1. Have your students sing and play the following exercise together in several keys.

2. Once comfortable with step 1 in several keys, have your students take turns improvising 1-2-3-5 shapes on C7. Do this over the first three beats of the measure (now indicated by slashes below).

Crucial Note: On this exercise your students MUST begin their improvisations on the 3rd of the V7 chord. In this case that means starting each improvised line on the pitch E (the 3rd of C7).

As before, give each student a chance. (While one student is improvising, the rest of the class alternates sings or plays the last two notes of the first measure—in this case B♭ to A.) Go around the whole class a few times. Again, there should be no stopping; they can handle some pressure to keep up.

Here are a few examples:

Some students may feel like they're in over their head with this step. By all means have the whole class play and sing the examples we've provided. This way, students having trouble will experience some success.

3. Repeat steps 1 and 2 in at least six keys.

As before, we recommend moving from key to key by descending whole steps. In harmony, this is called "downstep modulation" and is a really common harmonic motion in jazz. By going through your keys in this way, you'll be exposing your students to the sound of this important progression.

Lesson Plan 21: Using ♭7 to 3 Voice Leading to Improvise on II–7 | V7 | IΔ7

RECOMMENDED RECORDING, LESSON PLAN 21: BUD POWELL, *THE AMAZING BUD POWELL*. Recommended track: "Bouncing with Bud."

1. Have your students sing and play the following exercise together in several keys.

You might point out that this lesson plan simply combines the previous two.

2. As we did in the last two lesson plans, take turns improvising on 1-2-3-5 shapes when you see slashes. While one student is soloing, the rest of the class should alternate singing and playing the last two notes of each measure, every time.

Here are a few examples:

As before, give each student a few chances at this, moving through the whole class several times. And remember: no stopping. Keep in mind, this will likely feel like a tall order to your students. Choose helpful tempos, make lots of mistakes together, and keep the vibe playful.

3. Repeat steps 1 and 2 in at least six keys. As before, continue using the downstep modulation from the previous two lesson plans.

Teacher's Notes

SINGING BACKGROUNDS

To keep the class members involved while soloists take turns, you might have your students sing basic voicings as backgrounds. Start with just two notes (3 and 7), and follow the ♭7 to 3 voice leading through the progression:

If your students are more advanced, add the 5th and 9th to the voicing they sing:

No need for anything other than whole notes on these backgrounds; this is all about training your students to hear the progression.

TIPS FOR BUILDING 8TH-NOTE LINES

Some of your students may be ready to improvise more ambitious lines of their own. If this is the case, get them started by adding approach notes to the exercises. Start with the ♭7 to 3 resolution from Lesson Plan 18. Between each ♭7 and 3, add approach tones. For example:

Note that we approach the 3rd of C7 from below because it is major (see chapter 7). Next, add another chord tone out front, (in this case D—the 5th G–7), and give it an approach tone:

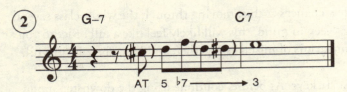

Finally, add another chord tone, this time B♭ (the 3rd), and give it a couple of approach tones from above:

With this process, you can keep extending an 8th-note line as far as you want. Repeat the process moving from V7 to IΔ7 and put it all together into a line covering the entire II–7 | V7 | IΔ7 progression.

RHYTHM SECTION

Piano/Guitar: Using Stepwise Motion

When voicing chords, make sure that your students move stepwise from one chord to the next rather than keeping the same shape in their hands and jumping around. Use common tones whenever possible. For example:

CHAPTER 13

II–7 | V7 | I (PART TWO)

Melodic Arpeggios and Dominant Cycles

Lesson Plan 22: Towards Improvising on II–7 | V7 | IΔ7

RECOMMENDED RECORDING, LESSON PLAN 22: CHARLIE PARKER AND DIZZY GILLESPIE, *DIZ 'N BIRD AT CARNEGIE HALL*. Recommended track: "Confirmation."

1. Have your students sing and play the following exercise together in several keys:

Invite your students to choose any octave that feels comfortable. In the first measure, let them choose whether they leap up from 3 to 5 or down from 3 to 5.

This might be a good opportunity to teach your students that a structure (such as a 3-5-7-9 arpeggio) does not change if you change the contour or even the note order. For example, 3-5-7-9 and 9-7-3-5 come from the same structure, just reordered. (If you feel your students won't understand yet, no need to say anything. Wait until a later time to explain it to them.)

2. Once your students are comfortable with step 1 in several keys, take turns improvising during the rests (indicated by slashes below) while the class continues playing step 1. As always, sing as often as you play.

For example:

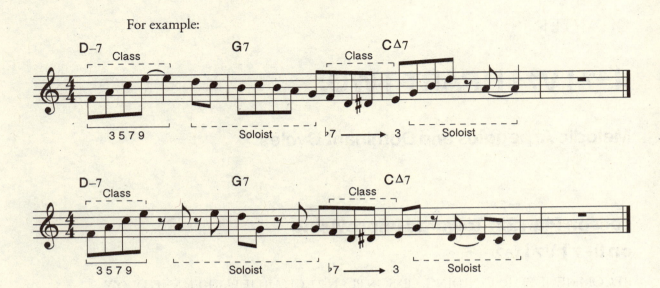

3. Repeat steps 1 and 2 in at least six keys.

Lesson Plan 23: Introducing #9 and ♭9 on the V7 Chord

RECOMMENDED RECORDING, LESSON PLAN 23: J.J. JOHNSON, *THE EMINENT JAY JAY JOHNSON*. Recommended track: "Get Happy."

1. Have your students sing and play the following exercise together in several keys:

As always, there's no need to explain the theory of #9 and ♭9 to your students. They just need to get used to the sound by playing it. You should also be aware that ♭9 resolves down to the 5th of the I chord. This is an extremely common resolution that jazz students should learn to hear early on.

2. Once your students are comfortable with step 1 in several keys, take turns improvising during the rests (indicated by slashes). Have the class continue playing step 1 while the soloist improvises:

For example:

In the above example, notice the use of chromatic approaches to the 3rd of D–7 (see Teacher's Notes, chapter 7).

Here's another example:

Note that, in the above examples, the soloist is simply improvising diatonically. The only altered pitches are the #9 and ♭9 in the second measure.

As before, have your whole class sing and play the "training wheels" from step 1 as your students take turns improvising. They're going to want to get away from the written notes, but don't let them yet! The discipline of this voice-leading will be critical once they are fully improvising on the II–7 | V7 | IΔ7.

Lesson Plan 24: Dominant Cycles (Part 1): 1-2-3-5 and 1-5-3-5

The cycle of ascending 4ths (descending 5ths) is the most common root movement in jazz harmony. The Dominant Cycle is a series of dominant chords that move around that cycle. (If you're unfamiliar with this root movement, don't worry—the examples that follow will make it clear.) These next few lesson plans give your students a few creative ways to practice this progression. This lesson plan is designed to help your students keep the chords in mind while they play. Do NOT let your students play this by ear; that's far too easy. *They must know what they're playing while they play it.*

Over the years, our students have gone to great lengths to avoid knowing what chords and notes they are actually playing while they improvise. It's how we know they're creative. Apparently, knowing what you're playing takes away that spontaneous magic. Oh well . . . hold them to it anyway. Below, you'll find examples of how to do that.

Before playing complicated lines on a dominant cycle, we start with easier material:

1. Have your students play 1-2-3-5 and 1-5-3-5, like this:

Note that the 1-2-3-5 is ascending (we'll label that "up"), and the 1-5-3-5 is descending (we'll label that "down").

2. Play each of these options over all 12 dominants, creating a stream of 8th-notes moving around the cycle of ascending 4ths.

If your students play 1-2-3-5 ("up") around the cycle, they get something that sounds like this:

And, if they play 1-5-3-5 ("down") around the cycle, they get this:

Your students need to be very comfortable with both of these before moving on.

Neither one of these options creates a satisfactory line alone. If your students only use one direction (either up or down), their transitions will be awkward every time they switch octaves. To create a smooth line, they need to combine *both* shapes (up and down) as they play through the cycle; see step 3).

3. Combine both shapes at random. Strive for no repeated patterns. Each chord should be connected by a whole-step (i.e. stepwise voice leading). Remember to *sing*. For example:

In terms of register, when you run out of room (either too high or too low), switch to the other option to change direction. Don't ever jump to the next root! By combining the two shapes in this way, your students will be able to create lines that weave through the cycle and change octaves smoothly.

To prevent being overly repetitive, don't just go back and forth between up and down. That's too predictable and doesn't involve enough choice. The line needs to be *unpredictable* (for example: down, up, up, down, down, up, up, up, down, etc.). *This means that your students must make a decision every two beats.* Exercises like these develop your students' ability to visualize (to picture what chords are coming in their mind's eye). As you speed up the exercise, it pushes their visualization further and further into the future.

The ability to mentally stay ahead of where one is playing—even if only by a chord or two—allows our motor skills to fire accurately while adapting to what's happening around us. Our brain "hiccups" when *what we play* catches up to *what we see coming*. In other words, when the point of execution gets too close to the point of visualization, the train comes to a screeching halt. At first, regardless of the tempo you choose, your students will likely stumble here and there. Don't stop to correct mistakes; let them practice keeping up, especially when they play something they didn't mean to.

By practicing these two shapes in tempo—with a metronome—your students will learn to ignore mistakes, keep going and show up on time for the next chord.

Lesson Plan 25: Dominant Cycles (Part 2): 3-5-7-9 Arpeggios

RECOMMENDED RECORDING, LESSON PLAN 25: CHARLIE PARKER AND DIZZY GILLESPIE, *TOGETHER*. Recommended track: "Shaw 'Nuff."

Jazz innovators like Charlie Parker and Sonny Rollins often organized their lines around an arpeggio starting on 3 and going up to 9. There are a number of solos played by Miles Davis that are extremely clear about this organization. It's obvious when you look at it, but not so obvious when you hear it. For example, he might play something like this:

In this example, the G7 is respelled as a D–7, and the line is organized between 9 and 3 of D–7. It starts on 9 (E), goes down to ♭3 (F), and then back up to 9 (E). You find this kind of organization almost everywhere in Miles's solos at that time. Later, his music became more abstract, but his feel for this kind of musical construction pervades even his most experimental playing.

This lesson plan will help your students build on the 3-5-7-9 sound from previous chapters. You want them to hear 3 and 9 as an important option for framing their lines.

1. Have your students sing and play the following at a slow tempo. *Do not be in a hurry*; they may have to repeat a bar or two here and there. It's important that the students *say* the name of the chord and the 3rd *before* they play it.

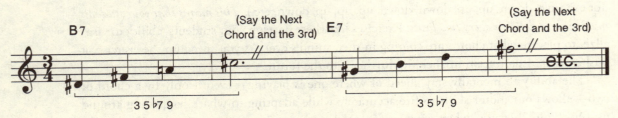

As an example, at the end of the second measure in the above example, your students would say, "E dominant, G sharp!" Do this all the way through the cycle until your students feel comfortable playing all twelve dominants in this way.

2. Repeat step 1, but "fold" the arpeggio by leaping *down* from 3 to 5. Don't forget to sing:

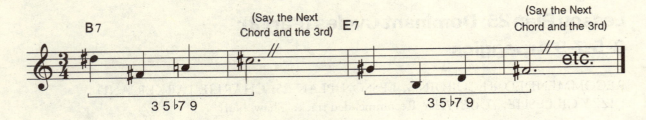

3. In 4/4, add the root and ♭7 to the previous 3-5-♭7-9. Do this slowly enough that they don't have to stop between chords. *Use a metronome and sing*.

To change register smoothly, just fold some arpeggios as needed. To make sure they don't just alternate between up and down, you might use hand gestures to keep the sequence unpredictable. (When you point up, they go from *3 up* to 5; when you point down, they go from *3 down* to 5.) You may have to stop here and there at first, but eventually, if you use a metronome to keep time, the class will visualize well enough to get through all twelve dominants without pausing.

3. Sing and play step 2 in 8th-notes instead of quarter notes. Because it's faster, start slowly and use a metronome to work the tempo up as we did in step 2.

This practice develops many critical skills: visualizing a structure regardless of differing shapes (folded and unfolded), looking ahead to the next chord and deciding which direction to go, developing a feel for creating smooth-flowing lines of 8th-notes, and developing the ability to hear cycles (even if they don't start on the root). And just as important: learning not to stop and bemoan mistakes.

Lesson Plan 26: Dominant Cycles (Part 3): Adding and Dropping Beats

RECOMMENDED RECORDING, LESSON PLAN 26: c. Recommended track: "Chi Chi (Take 6/Master)."

Young jazz musicians need the ability to play lines that move back and forth across barlines. That said, the next two lesson plans may be a tad too advanced for your students. If they seem too difficult, feel free to move on to the next chapter and save these for a later time.

On the other hand, if your students are ready for the content of these next lesson plans, they will find them tremendously helpful.

1. The following melodic line adds two approach tones to the 3rd of each dominant. Sing and play through the entire cycle.

Just as in Lesson Plan 25, you change direction by how you play the first two notes of each arpeggio. (If 3 leaps *down* to 5, the shape goes down; if 3 leaps *up* to 5, the line goes up. As before, direct the class with your hands, pointing up or down.)

Continue this pattern until they have played this shape through all 12 dominants. Remind your students that the voice-leading from ♭7 to 3 is what makes the chords sound like they are moving.

2. How to "drop a beat." Have your students sing and play the melodic line from step 1 again. This time, take out the chromatic approaches on one chord. *On one chord only.* By taking out these approaches *on one chord only*, each subsequent chord will be played one beat early. We call this "dropping a beat." Each chord will continue to be early (by one beat) until you decide to add back a beat (see steps 3 and 4).

The rhythm section must comp along so that your students can hear how this new line relates to the meter. If the rhythm section isn't available you can use a play-along recording or app. The most important thing is to hear the bass against the line. We recommend having the bassist play four quarter notes on each root. It's the best thing to help the students feel how monumental "dropping a beat" really is.

Dropping a beat is another way to practice anticipating the next chord, creating a feeling of always moving forward. Students tend to resolve their lines at the barline. As a result, their playing often sounds pedantic, as though they are playing station to station. By contrast, when they anticipate, it feels as though they are taking the whole band forward with them.

3. How to "add a beat." Have your students play the melodic line from step 2 again. This time— on one chord only—*add* two approaches that surround the root with chromatic pitches:

We call this "adding a beat." By adding these approaches to B7 (measure 1 in the example), you are now playing the 3rd of E7 one beat later. Each subsequent chord will be one beat late until you drop a beat and make the chords line up again (see step 4).

4. Randomly drop and add beats around the dominant cycle. If the 3rd of each chord has been arriving early (on beat four instead of beat 1), "adding a beat" straightens things out by returning the chord change to beat one. On the other hand, if the 3rds have been sounding on time (*on* beat one), "adding" a beat will make them arrive one beat later on beat two. For example:

Take a look at the example above. We drop a beat in measure 2, which places the 3rd of the next chord (F7) one beat earlier (beat 4 of that same measure). As a result, the 3rd of B♭7 also arrives early (beat 4, measure 3). Then, in measure 4, we add a beat, returning the 3rd of E♭7 to beat 1 (measure 5). Next (also in measure 5) we add another beat, causing each subsequent chord change to sound one beat later (beat 2 of measures 6, 6, and 8). We straighten out again by dropping a beat in measure 8, and so on.

As you drop and add beats together, you might create simple hand signals as a way to conduct each option (add or drop). You will likely need to cue them an entire measure early for your students to successfully respond. Keep your students on their toes with this game. *Be unpredictable.*

Lesson Plan 27: 3-5-7-9 + Approach Tones: Dropping and Adding Beats on II–7 | V7 | IΔ7

RECOMMENDED RECORDING, LESSON PLAN 27: CHET BAKER, *CHET BAKER QUARTET FEATURING RUSS FREEMAN*. Recommended track: "Happy Little Sunbeam."

1. Have your students sing and play the following exercise in several keys:

Note: In this example, the 9th of G7 is lowered. The ♭9 is an extremely common sound in jazz and can be used on any dominant chord that moves to a I chord of some kind (IΔ7, I7, or I–7).

Note that the arpeggio on the IΔ7 is "folded" (it leaps *down* from 3 to 5). As with Lesson Plan 26, you can "fold" any of these 3-5-7-9 arpeggios. We recommend practicing this with the down-step modulation from before. As a reminder:

D–7 | G7 | CΔ7
C–7 | F7 | B♭Δ7
B♭–7 | E♭7 | A♭Δ7
And so on . . . .

Remember, this down-step modulation will only take your students through six keys. To get to all twelve, modulate up one half-step after they play their sixth key and repeat the sequence. Because they have the option of folding any 3-5-7-9 arpeggio, no part of this phrase should be too high or too low for your students.

2. After singing and playing step 1 in several keys, have your students drop the approaches from the first bar (the two notes in parentheses), as in the *second* example below.

The original line:

The same line with the approaches dropped from measure 1:

Sing and play this rhythmically offset version of the line in several keys. Point out that dropping a beat in this way moves the 3rd of the next chord earlier by one beat. This has the effect of *anticipating* the next chord (G7 in this case). Anticipating in this way gives your line more momentum. Remember: *if you're not early, you're late.*

3. After singing and playing step 2 (together) in several keys, have your students drop the approaches from the *second* bar instead:

The original line:

The same line with the approaches dropped from measure *2*:

As in step 2, sing and play this offset version of the line in several keys. Point out that this example shifts the 3rd of C△7 one beat earlier, this time *anticipating* the I△7 chord.

4. After singing and playing step 3 (together) in several keys, have your students *add one beat* to measure one by surrounding the root with chromatic approaches. They can also add one beat to measure two by adding a ♯9.

The original line:

The same line with one beat added to measure 1:

The same line with one beat added to measure 2.

These examples have the opposite effect of steps 2 and 3. Instead of *anticipating* the sound of the next chord by one beat, they *delay* the chord change by one beat.

5. Once your students are comfortable with steps 1 through 4 in several keys, play the following game together, designed to allow them to choose what comes next:
   • Choose one of the options from steps 1, 2, 3, or 4, and play it together in time.
   • While resting in tempo, let your students take turns calling out which variation the class will play next (seen in quotation marks above rests in the following example).
   • Repeat.

For example:

As in the example above, you might have your students modulate to a new key every few repetitions. If this is too much for them right now, stay in the same key for as long as is needed. As a reminder, if you add a beat to the dominant measure, use ♯9 ♭9 as in step 4 above.

CHAPTER 14

PLAYING THE BLUES (PART 1)

We realize we're running up against a time-honored tradition in jazz education by waiting until now to address the blues. No disrespect meant. The blues—the form, feel, phrasing and language—are more central to jazz than any other influence. Whenever we hear someone say, "It's just a blues," we know they don't understand jazz. To us, that's kind of like saying of a painting, "It's just a Rembrandt." As we said earlier, the blues is not just a part of jazz, it makes jazz what it is. Despite this, we feel it may not be the best place to start teaching students to improvise.

Why We Didn't Start with the Blues

Over our shared 54 years of teaching jazz, we've heard thousands of students who have been introduced to improvising by playing a blues. By and large, they move up and down a blues scale (1, ♭3, 4, ♯4, 5, ♭7) without regard to harmony, phrasing, or form, and without getting much of the *feeling* of this pivotal music.

As jazz musicians, we spend a lifetime studying the blues. And running up and down a blues scale without tipping your hat to the form—harmonically, lyrically, and historically—is not playing jazz. As the teacher, this is not your fault. Starting with the blues in this way has been passed down and accepted as the wisest, most genuine way of starting to play jazz.

What the Blues Means to Us

Students gain a better grasp of the blues when they learn where the music comes from. To that end, here are some of our thoughts regarding the origin and meanings of this extraordinary music.

Under dire circumstances, when human beings have few possessions, what little they have often comes to mean as much as life itself. As the poet Michael Longley* pointed out, "In the ashes outside the crematoria in Auschwitz, they discovered scraps of poems" as well as music. Faced with the unimaginable, it becomes clear what matters most—what truly makes us human.

It was no different with the horrors of chattel slavery in the United States. Here, enslaved people greatly outnumbered their enslavers. As a result, those profiting from chattel slavery wanted their human "property" to be docile and accepting of their lot. It was commonly believed that if the enslaved were singing, they were happy, and therefore less likely to revolt. As a result, music (particularly singing) was one of the only activities that was allowed and even encouraged.

---

* See *The On Being Project*, "Michael Longley: The Vitality of Ordinary Things."

However, in many cases, the songs created did not express this presumed happiness. Rather they were filled with a wide range of human experience: sorrow, misery, frustration, spirituality, hope, and humor. Often, the songs also carried a carefully coded derision of their oppressors, and an even more carefully coded desire for revolution, justice, and a determination to maintain identity. Out of this came the blues (and, later, jazz).

It's no accident that one of the things people find most attractive about the blues and jazz is the remarkable freedom that they give to those who play. It's the kind of freedom that says one need not play the same thing the same way twice; the freedom to express non-verbal feelings in ways that may, in other contexts, be socially unacceptable and even illegal (as is so often the case with truth-telling amid unjust laws).

The blues were developed by a people expressing themselves in the only ways that were available to them, ways that wouldn't get them murdered. To quote Dizzy Gillespie, people "died for this music. You can't get more serious than that."*

Yet, although the blues often deals with sad things, *it is not sad music.* Meanings in the blues are rarely reflected on the surface of the lyrics. You've got to go deeper than the surface to find what matters in this music. Blues can be uplifting, profound, spiritual, humorous, and ironic—*especially* when the words seem sad. As Albert Murray wrote, when we play with the tragi-comic experiences of life, we shift our relationship to those experiences, stylizing and humanizing of the chaos of living."†

The blues reflects the indomitable will of its creators, the refusal to lose even in the face of defeat; an implacable determination that this will someday be over, that evil and injustice will not win in the end. It is a repository for feelings left unsaid. As such, jazz and blues are cultural vessels with resilience in their very DNA; resilience born of a profound understanding of freedom.

Duke Ellington named the freedoms he heard at the heart of the music (specifically, in the life and music of his closest collaborator, Billy Strayhorn):

Freedom from hate, unconditionally.
Freedom from all self-pity (even throughout all the pain and bad news).
Freedom from the fear of possibly doing something that might help another more
 than it would help himself.
Freedom from the kind of pride that could make a man feel he was better than his
 brother or neighbor.††

It has become popular to retell the origin story of the blues and jazz as though their most important values came from American democracy. We see a danger in this. Knowingly or not, those retelling the story of the blues this way risk saying that enslaved African Americans (and their descendants) could never have created such profound art without the influence of European-American thought. But remember, chattel slavery held a central place in both colonial American democracy and the thought that inspired it.

In our view, the blues—and jazz by extension—did not come from a political system, inspired by European thought, and designed largely by those propagating chattel slavery in the

---

* Grover Sales, "The Immortal Joker: Part Two," *Gene Lees Jazzletter* 18, no. 3 (1999): 5.
† Albert Murray, *The Omni-Americans* (New York: Da Capo, 1970), 58.
†† Duke Ellington, *Music Is My Mistress*, (New York: Da Capo, 1973), 159–61.

United States. Unequivocally—inarguably—it was the response of Black Americans to chattel slavery (and its aftermath) that led to the creation of this extraordinary music.

These musicians' understanding of personhood and freedom lies at the heart of blues and jazz. That insight didn't come from those in power; it came *despite* them.

What was created was *not* just a niche music. It broke things open that needed to be broken open; it's everybody's music. The musicians who created this music realized it was bigger than the constrictions of a national identity. As Dizzy Gillespie said, "We never wished to be restricted to just an American context, for we were creators in an art form which grew from universal roots, and which had proved that it had universal appeal."[*]

Knowing something of the origin and meanings of the blues changes our relationship with it. The deeper we go, the more we realize that we'll never get to the bottom of it. We also realize what a treasure it is—a music carrying human values affirmed amidst the most trying of circumstances; values which, in the minds of those artists who created it, grew from universal roots. To our perception, the global influence of the blues seems to support this.

As with all culture, the values embodied by this remarkable music are never more than a generation away from the risk of disappearing. It's up to all of us to pass them along. We invite you to help your students understand the cultural and emotional power of this music; its reason for being. To assist in this effort, we highly recommend the writings of, among others, Ralph Ellison, Albert Murray, James Baldwin, Eric Porter, Ingrid Monson, Maya Angelou, Stanley Crouch, Travis Jackson, Toni Morrison, and Robert O'Meally.

Lesson Plan 28: Using Approach Tones to Hear the Harmonic Form of the Blues (Less Advanced)

The first two lesson plans in this chapter (Lesson Plans 28 and 29) are designed for your students once they have gained some basic skill with the materials from chapters 2 and 3. Lesson Plan 28 lays the foundation for hearing the harmonic form of the blues and is designed for students with limited experience. More advanced students will absorb the material quickly but should not skip it.

Before we improvise on the blues, your students must learn to hear what it really sounds like. To this end, we have chosen to begin with the harmonic form of the blues. Lesson Plan 28 is designed for ear training and improving visualization, and has no steps involving choice or improvisation. These exercises will also give your students some basic building blocks for improvising on the blues when the time comes.

---

[*] Eric Porter, *What Is This Thing Called Jazz*, (Berkeley: University of California Press, 2002), 59.

1. Show your students the 12-bar blues form (below). Have the class sing the roots of each chord several times until the sequence sounds familiar to them. After singing several times, *play* through the roots. This is fairly simple, so you can alternate singing and playing if you like.

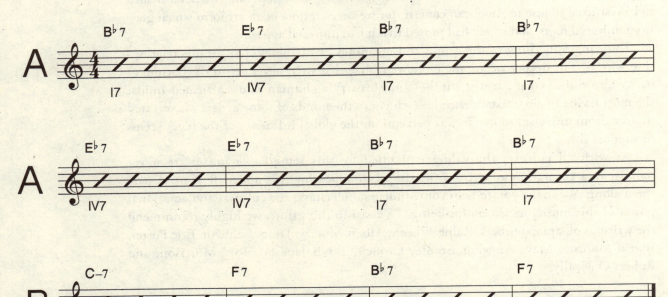

This example has the basic harmonic framework of a blues in B♭, with Roman numerals underneath each bar to help you transpose as needed. The A-A-B written on the left side of the example has nothing to do with the harmony. Rather, it refers to a melodic form that comes from the lyrics. We will get to that in the next chapter. For now, you might mention to your students that A-A-B means, "Say Something (A), Say it Again (A), Comment on what's been said (B)." Sing the roots of each chord with a play-along track or with the rhythm section comping. Do this until the class can do it in their sleep.

PLAYING THE BLUES (PART 1)   117

2. Play the following example for your students and have them sing it back until they have it *memorized*. This is just approaching the root of each chord from two half-steps below. When they're ready, play through it as well.

3. As in step 2, play the following example for your students and have them sing it back until they have it *memorized*. This step approaches the root of each chord from two half-steps above. When they're ready, play through it as well.

4. *Again*, play this and have your students *sing* it back until they have it. It approaches the 3rd of each chord and, most important, respells IV7 and V7 (see chapter 11 for a refresher on respelling if needed):

We respell the IV7 and V7 chords to make playing on the blues as easy as possible, and to hopefully have better results than we usually hear. As you can see above, this means that E♭7 becomes B♭–7, and F7 becomes C–7 (for a review of respelling, see chapter 11). Doing this gives the student only three chords to learn and to hear in their proper place, while preserving the sound of the blues progression. Memorization is key to learning any chord progression. When we say this, we mean memorizing the *sound* and not just a sequence of chord names. Anyone can learn a list of chord names, but *without knowing the sound it doesn't mean a thing*.

PLAYING THE BLUES (PART 1)   119

5. As before, have your students *sing* and play the following example until they have it *memorized*. We're only adding two notes here—approaches to the 3rd of E♭7 (see measure 5) and the 3rd of F7 (see measure 10). Note that measure 10 approaches both the 3rd and 7th of F7:

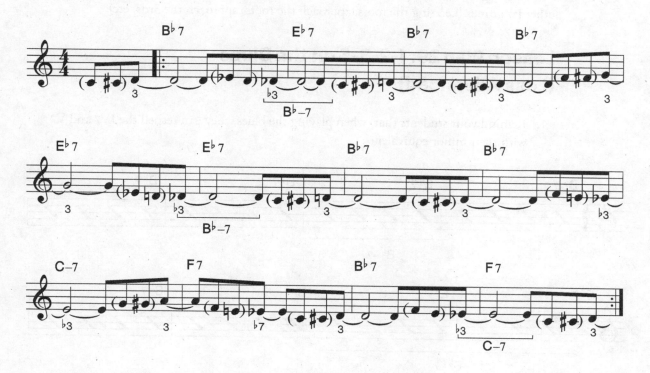

6. Once again, have your students *sing* and play this until it's *memorized*. This final step adds a G7 in measure 8 (in roman numerals, a dominant VI7 or V7/II–7):

The VI7 in measure 8 is a pivotal sound when playing a jazz blues but is not found often in rock or traditional blues.

Get familiar with all these options. *Mix and match* them as many ways as you can.

The steps for learning to hear blues harmonies work equally well for the harmonies in other jazz tunes (i.e., sing the roots, approach the roots, approach the 3rds, etc).

Lesson Plan 29: 1-2-3-5 on the Blues (Less Advanced)

1. Remind your students that, when playing the blues, they can respell the IV7 and V7 with their minor equivalents:

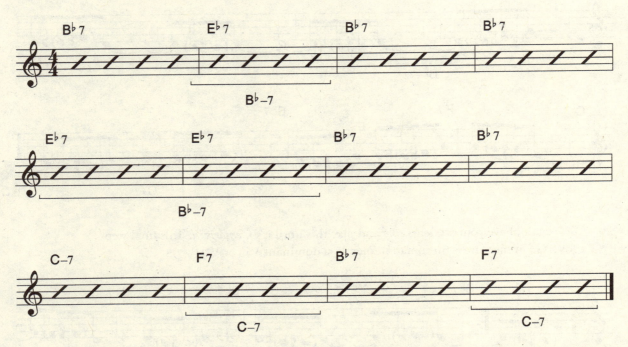

The respellings are written below each measure. With these respellings, there are only three chords for your students to think about: B♭7, B♭–7 and C–7.

PLAYING THE BLUES (PART 1)   121

2. Apply chapters 2 and 3 (root triads and 1-2-3-5 shapes) to each chord from the respelling (i.e., B♭7, B♭–7 and C–7).

Before playing on the actual blues form, isolate two of these chords and move back and forth between them while improvising on the 1-2-3-5 shape. In the example below, we demonstrate practicing B♭7 and B♭–7. At first, play each chord for four measures each, then two measures each. For example:

After you've done this with B♭7 and B♭–7, repeat the process moving from C–7 to B♭7.

3. To reinforce the sound of these respellings on the blues form, have your students sing and play the following blues head over and over again until it's memorized.

You could have some members of the class play this, while others take turns improvising along with it. Another useful option is to alternate between playing this blues head and having soloists improvise.

4. Let your students take turns improvising with 1-2-3-5 shapes on the blues form, using the minor respellings on E♭7 and F7:

Have the class play each one of the variations from Lesson Plan 28 and use it as an interlude between improvised solos. Let each soloist improvise twice through the 12-bar form. It should look like this:

- The entire class plays variation 1 (see step 2, Lesson Plan 28).
- Student #1 plays a solo for 12 bars while the rhythm section comps on the form.
- The class plays variation 2 (see step 3, Lesson Plan 28).
- Student #1 plays another solo for 12 bars.
- And so on . . .

The class should play all five variations from Lesson Plan 28 over the course of this exercise. You can pick which ones, or just have them play the variations in order. Remember, the soloists improvise on the simplified respellings of the chords (so that they are only thinking of B♭7, B♭–7 and C–7), even though the rest of the class is sometimes playing a more complex version of the harmony.

Teacher's Notes

HARMONIC OPTIONS ON THE BLUES

As your students get more experienced, there are a few more harmonic options on the blues you should know about. In measure 6 we introduce two chords: IV–7 and ♭VII7 (E♭–7 A♭7) before returning to I, which is now major as opposed to dominant (B♭∆7). And, measure 8 now has two chords as well: IIIø and VI7alt (Dø G7alt):

```
Mea.   1      2       3      4
    || B♭7 | E♭7  |  F–7  | B♭7
       5       6         7         8
     E♭7 | E♭–7 A♭7 | B♭∆7 | Dø G7alt
       9    10    11      12
     C–7 | F7 | B♭7 | C–7 F7 ||
```

THE TURNAROUND

It's common to play another progression in the last two measures of the form (measures 11–12):

```
Mea. 11        12
  || I∆7 VI7 | II–7 V7 ||
```

Jazz musicians call this a turnaround because it makes a U-turn and goes back to the beginning of the form. "Turnaround" also refers to any variation on this progression. Common variations include:

|| III–7 VI7 | II–7 V7 ||

|| I∆7 ♭III7 | ♭VI7 ♭II7 ||

Either of these options can show up in measures 11–12.

RHYTHM SECTION

Piano: An Example of Comping on the Blues

Here's an example of comping on a blues with four-note voicings, using the chord progression from Lesson Plan 29.

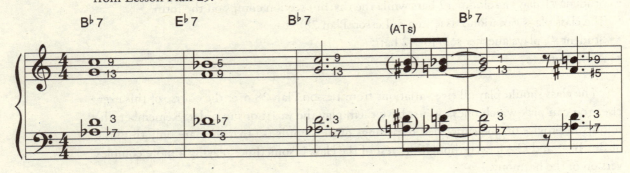

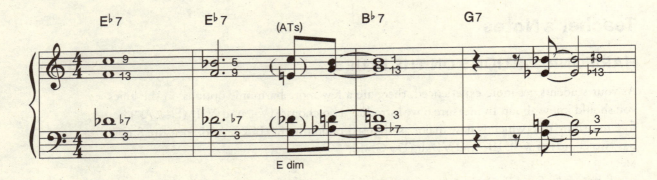

CHAPTER 15

THE VOCAL FORM OF THE BLUES

While the previous chapter prepared your students to hear the harmonic form of the blues, in this chapter, we turn our attention to how the lyrics influence blues melodies and form. If students don't know some standard blues lyrics, they won't see the reason for the blues form being what it is, and certainly won't have a feel for it. You may notice that there are fewer written examples in this chapter. This is 100 percent by design. We will keep coming back to this throughout this chapter, but it's worth saying right from the outset: *the material in this chapter **needs** to be learned by ear and repeated until it is internalized by heart.*

Lesson Plan 30: Introducing the Vocal Form of the Blues (Less Advanced)

1. Listen to Joe Williams perform "Everyday I Have the Blues" with the Count Basie Orchestra. We recommend the live performance at Carnegie Hall in 1981, which you can find on Youtube. The vocals start at about 1:10.

Note that the lyrics follow an A-A-B form:

> Everyday I have the blues. (A)
> Everyday I have the blues. (A)
> When you see me worry, baby, it's you I hate to lose. (B)
> Nobody loves me, nobody seems to care (A)
> Nobody loves me, nobody seems to care (A)
> Speaking of bad luck and trouble, you note that I have my share. (B)

And so on.

Another great example is "Alright, Okay, You Win," also performed by Joe Williams with the Count Basie Orchestra.

> Alright, okay, you win, I'm in love with you (A)
> Alright, okay, you win, I'm in love with you (A)
> I'll do anything you say, it's just got to be that way. (B)

In both of these examples, the lyrics create an A-A-B form: say something (A), say it again with variation (A), say something different (B). Note that the melody on the second A-section changes slightly, even though the words are the same as the first A-section. Point out that each section of the form is four measures long, just like the harmonic form you have been practicing.

2. Choose one of the tunes from step 1, and have the class sing along with the vocals over and over again until they have it *memorized*.

Have your students try to memorize the words *and* the phrasing, including any expressive effects (bent notes, etc.) Most important: capture the feeling portrayed by the artist.

Critical Note: When you ask students to imitate Joe Williams' phrasing, you must be careful not to let them get stuck on surface gestures. Focus on feeling, timing, and phrasing.

The goal is always to find an honest emotional connection to the music, *not a superficial caricature.* We have seen some students (knowingly or unknowingly) present racial caricatures of the artists they imitate. This subject is somewhat controversial, to put it mildly, but our objective in those moments is to teach students about the pain caused by such caricatures.

3. After your students learn to sing the melody, have them try to phrase like Joe Williams *on their instruments*. They will likely not be too successful at this point, because this kind of thing takes time. Repeat this until you feel they have begun to get closer to Joe Williams' style and feel.

Tell your students not to be afraid to fail dozens and dozens (or even hundreds) of times as they try to mimic the blues voice on their instruments. In some educational circles, they might be encouraged to *practice perfection* in order to play perfectly. *Jazz is not like that.* Because we constantly work on new challenges and create lines that we haven't practiced, our playing will always be imperfect. If your students embrace this early on, they will be set up for a lifetime of growing as an artist without fear of failure. As the legendary brass teacher, Carmine Caruso, was fond of saying, "We learn to walk by falling."

4. Write a set of blues lyrics together. This might seem a little "young," but we've had success doing this with students of all ages.

Follow this form:

(A) State a problem
(A) Repeat the problem (maybe with an extra word or two)
(B) Comment on the problem, whether it gets worse or better

Example:

"Springtime's here, and I'm still stuck in school. (A)
"Springtime's here, and I'm still stuck in school. (A)
"Teacher says it matters, but I think he's a fool. (B)

"My parents have a Benz, but never let me drive. (A)
"My parents have a big ol' Benz, but never let me drive. (A)
"When I can buy my own, I'm gonna buy me five." (B)

5. Invite a few daring students to perform your new blues, improvising their own melody as they sing the words you wrote. You might choose a soloist or two to do call and response with the vocals, like this:

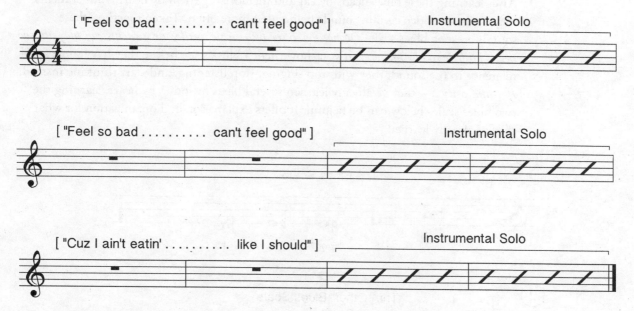

The rhythm section should comp over the harmonic form of the 12-bar blues as they did in the last chapter. (If your students are like ours, it will take some practice getting comfortable with leaving space for four measures to pass before they sing the second "A," and then the following "B." *Don't move on until leaving space feels like home.*)

Lesson Plan 31: Instrumental Blues (Part 1—Less Advanced)

1. Listen to Freddie Hubbard performing the head to *Blues for Duane* several times. (The "head" is the term jazz musicians use for the composed melody that is played at the beginning of a tune, before improvising begins. More often than not, it returns again at the end of the piece.)
2. Have your students sing along until they have it *memorized*. You might have them make a loop of it, repeating it ad infinitum.
3. Once your students can sing it, have them play the melody along with Freddie Hubbard and try to phrase on their instruments just as they did when they sang it. Point out that this head emphasizes the same pitches that we did back in Lesson Plan 29, just in a different key (F).
4. "Blues for Duane" is very easy. Play it in several keys.
5. Repeat steps 1 through 4 with "Sonnymoon for Two" as performed by Sonny Rollins.
6. Repeat steps 1 through 4 with "Work," performed by Sonny Rollins.
7. Repeat steps 1 through 4 with "Bag's Groove," performed by Miles Davis (1954). If they're up to it, your students might also learn the harmony line played by vibraphonist Milt Jackson.

8. Repeat steps 1 through 4 with "Splanky," performed by Count Basie on the album "Atomic Basie." Have them learn the head (which begins at about 0:13) and—very important—the 24-bar shout chorus (which begins at about 1:45).
9. After learning these blues heads by ear and memorizing them by heart, your students may begin to notice certain sounds being used more often. Taken together, these sounds create a blues scale. *Do not touch the blues scale until your students can play all five heads proficiently by memory.* If you show them a blues scale before they have some aural reference to the sound, they will stop singing, stop listening, and start thinking instead. *If—and **only** if—*they've already learned several blues melodies by heart, learning the two blues scales below can be helpful. It offers explanation and organization for what they've already learned.

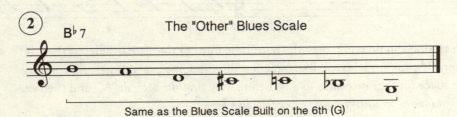

Both of these scales represent a set of pitches used to create blues melodies. They are both written as they would be used in the key of B♭. Note that the "Other Blues Scale" is actually a G blues scale (a blues scale built on the 6th of the key). *Both of these are used all of the time.*

Here are a couple of melodies that come from each of these blues scales:

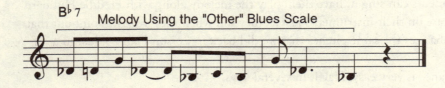

10. Have your students improvise on the blues, using the information they've gleaned from all of the heads they learned.

Your students' goal is to improvise a solo that sounds like a composed blues head.

Insist that your students play solos that stick to the A-A-B lyric form. In other words, play a phrase on the first four bars (A), repeat it or play something very much like it on the second four bars (A), then play something different on the last four bars (B). *Do not let them wander away from this until it feels second nature to them.* After learning several heads in their original key by ear, *it can be helpful to transpose all of them to a single key*, like B♭ or F, so that your students have immediate access to those sounds when they improvise. The process for learning like this never changes:

1) Have your students learn a new head by heart.
2) Play it over and over and over again (in more than one key).
3) When they get back to improvising, try to use the head in their solos.

Students might start by changing little parts of the head as they go, or perhaps trading fours with the head (play four measures of the head, then improvise four, etc.).

Lesson Plan 32: Instrumental Blues (Part 2—Less Advanced)

Here are three blues heads by John McNeil, composed for this book. We took pains to make them fairly consistent as to their use of the two blues scales and some harmony from earlier lessons. They combine some things in new ways (there are a few surprises), but you'll be able to understand the contents using the information you now have (John is laughing now . . . .)

1. Have your students sing the following blues head until they have it memorized. Once they can sing it, have them play it in a few keys.

Stop Bothering Me

Point out the following: (1) The melodic form of this blues is A-A-A. The last "A" section is a little bit different than the first two; (2) The phrases are clearly four measures long; (3) Most of the pitches come from the blues scale (any that don't can be understood as approaches).

2. Once again, have your students sing this until they have it memorized. Once they can sing it, have them play it in a few keys.

Copacetic

Be sure your pianist/guitarist catches the B7sus chord in the last measure (just have them voice the respelling; in this case, F# minor with B in the bass).

3. One more time, have your students sing this until they have it memorized. Once they can sing it, have them play it in a few keys.

Listen Here

This head introduces a more surprising combination of sounds. No need to explain them. Just let your students get some of these sounds swimming around in their ears by singing and playing.

Lesson Plan 33: Instrumental Blues (Part 3—More Advanced)

As a form and a mode of expression, the blues evolved as it interacted with every major jazz artist. We cannot possibly give an exhaustive treatment of this extraordinary music. Here are several incredibly important innovators in jazz, with a list of tunes/albums to check out as your students deepen their roots in the blues. With any of these tunes, focus on learning the heads. Don't worry about learning entire solos yet.

Many of these tunes are complex enough that you will likely need some way to slow down the recordings so that your students can hear the pitches more accurately. There are several wonderful apps available that can do this. We have enjoyed using "Transcribe," "Amazing Slow Downer," and "Anytune."

1. Choose one track from the list below. Have your students listen to the head over and over again while trying to *sing* along.
2. Have them try to *play* along. Perhaps alternate singing and playing. If needed, slow the track down so that your students can figure out every note.
3. Transpose the new head to some other keys, including any keys from your repertoire.
4. Repeat steps 1 through 3 on several other heads.
5. Have your students improvise, striving to create a solo while keeping the head in mind as they play. You might play a game where every time you snap your fingers, they go from improvising back to singing the head. Great exercise!

List of Blues Tunes

Geri Allen: "Vanguard Blues (Live)"
Joanne Brackeen: "Knickerbocker Blues" and "C-Sri"
Clifford Brown: "Sandu," "The Double Up," and "Blues Walk"
John Coltrane: The entire album, *John Coltrane Plays the Blues* (1962), especially the track, "Blues to You"; also (from other albums) "Bessie's Blues," "Blue Trane," and "Some Other Blues"
Miles Davis: "Walkin'," "Trane's Blues," "Blues by Five," "Dr. Jekyll" (by Jackie McLean), "Down," "Eighty-One" (by Wayne Shorter), "Cheryl," "Sippin' at Belle's," "Somethin' Else," and "Pfrancing"
Duke Ellington and John Coltrane: "Take the Coltrane"
Duke Ellington: "Things Ain't What They Used to Be," "Diminuendo and Crescendo in Blue," and *Blues in Orbit (*album). Blues tracks from *Blues in Orbit*: "Three J's Blues," "Pie's Eye's Blues," "Sweet and Pungent," "C Jam Blues," "Blues in Blueprint," "The Swingers Get the Blues Too," "The Swinger's Jump," and "Blues in Orbit"
Joe Henderson: "Tetragon," "Isotope," and "Homestretch"
Freddie Hubbard: "Hub-Tones" and "Birdlike"
Melba Liston: "Blues Melba"
Jackie McLean: *Bluesnik* (album). Blues tracks from *Bluesnik*: "Bluesnik," "Goin' Way Blues," "Drew's Blues," and "Blues Function"
Charles Mingus: *Blues and Roots* (album). Blues tracks from *Blues and Roots*: "Wednesday Night Prayer Meeting," "Cryin' Blues," and "E's Flat Ah's Flat Too." See also "II B.S"
Hank Mobley: "My Groove," "Your Move"
Thelonious Monk: "Blue Monk," "Straight No Chaser," "Ba-lue Bolivar," "Ba-lues Are," and "Misterioso"

Charlie Parker: "Blue Bird," "Now's the Time," "Au Privave," "Billie's Bounce," "Bloomdido," "Blues for Alice," "K.C. Blues," "Laird Baird," "Parker's Mood," "Air Conditioning," "Chi Chi," "Visa," "Bongo Beep," "Bongo Bop," "Si Si, Relaxin' at Camarillo," "Mohawk," and "Bird Feathers"
Bud Powell: "Dance of the Infidels"
Sonny Rollins: "Blues for Philly Joe," "Blue 7," "Work," "Sonnymoon for Two," and "Bluesnote"
Sonny Rollins and John Coltrane: "Tenor Madness"
Shirley Scott: "Soul Shoutin'"
Woody Shaw: "Blues for Wood"
Horace Silver: "Blowin' the Blues Away," "Baghdad Blues," "Cape Verdean Blues," and "Señor Blues"
Clark Terry: "Blues for Smedley," "The Hymn," and *Yes, the Blues* (entire album)
Mary Lou Williams: "The Blues"

For historical context, we also recommend:

Louis Armstrong: From *Louis Armstrong Plays W.C. Handy* (album): "St. Louis Blues," "Yellow Dog Blues," "Aunt Hagar's Blues," and "Hesitating Blues." See also "West End Blues"

Teacher's Notes

RHYTHM SECTION

Recommended Blues Tracks for Piano

There are some unique devices that pianists use to imitate blues inflections. To that end, here are a few good places to start in order to help your students:

Oscar Peterson and Count Basie: "Slow Blues"
Ray Brown Trio: "The Real Blues" (From the album, *Summerwind*)
Miles Davis Quintet: "Freddie Freeloader" (with Wynton Kelly on piano), "Trane's Blues, No Blues" (also called "Pfrancing"), "Straight No Chaser," and "Blues by Five" (with Red Garland on piano)

We also recommend checking out Mary Lou Williams, Oscar Peterson, Sonny Clark, Herbie Hancock, Duke Ellington, Thelonious Monk, Horace Silver, and Gene Harris to get a feel for how to approach blues inflections on the piano.

CHAPTER 16

A GUIDE TO TRANSCRIBING (LEARNING BY EAR)

Transcribing is a critical part of any jazz musician's development. When jazz musicians say "transcribing," they mean imitating recorded solos by ear and learning them by heart. We often write down the solo as well in order to figure out what makes it tick, just as novice painters routinely copy paintings of the great masters to improve their skills. Some students (particularly younger students) feel concerned that if they imitate another artist by transcribing, it might hurt their originality. *This simply isn't true.* Rather than making the transcriber less original, imitation can have the same effect that stimulating conversation has on a writer.

Getting Started

Jumping into transcribing can feel like drinking from a fire hose. A few preparatory steps make it a lot easier.

1) **Listen to the solo ten times in a row.** No need to listen to the whole track, just loop the solo. The students don't even need to think about it; just listen uncritically.
2) **Try to sing along.** Another ten times will do. Your students won't succeed in keeping up with the soloist, but simply making the attempt brings them closer to the sound, shape and spirit of the solo.
3) **Figure out how long the solo is.** Have them mark off some manuscript paper with the appropriate number of bars. Number the beginning of each chorus (a chorus is one time through the harmonic/melodic form of a tune).

    Psychologically, this makes a big difference. Once students have the bars marked off for the entire solo, it feels like all they have to do is fill them in!
4) **Figure out the solo on their instruments.** Students may need to do this one note at a time and will almost certainly need to slow down the recording so that they can hear each pitch accurately. We recommend apps or software such as the Amazing Slow Downer, Transcribe, Anytune or others to slow down the music and make it more accessible. A simple internet search will help you find one of the many programs out there. As your students figure out the solo, have them write it down.

    If they find a measure or two that doesn't yield easily, tell them to give it four or five tries and then move on. When they're done, they might wind up with a half-dozen (or more) empty bars in their written transcription. At that point, they can go back and figure out a particular measure from both sides (i.e., how does the solo enter the measure, how does it leave the measure). If they can't get the rhythms, they can just write out the note heads. If they can't get the notes, write the rhythms.

    Always, the most important thing is learning the entire performance by heart.

Sometimes, a student just can't figure out a passage. Tell them not to worry about it. They can always come back again in a couple of years and sort it out.

5) **Analyze the transcription.** Help students write in chord changes above the appropriate measures. Using what you've learned in this book, figure out the relationship between the notes and the written chords (see below for several examples of this).

If you and your students have difficulty recognizing the chords on a given tune, you can find them in fakebooks or other resources (such as contacting a local jazz musician). Fakebooks often have inaccuracies on each tune but can still be a useful place to start. Most jazz musicians love the art form enough to care about passing it on; they can be great resources for checking chords on tunes.

Once ready, try to figure out the chords by listening to a recording. At the very least, concentrate on the bass to get a sense of what it is playing at the beginning of each bar. Between the solo and the bass notes, you can probably figure out a fair amount of the harmony. This may take some time, but students who are serious about learning the music will want to start this process early. (Pro-tip: Sometimes jazz musicians play structures that explicitly indicate harmonies *different from the written chords*. If you see a structure that doesn't seem to correspond with the written chord, you've probably stumbled across something new to practice.)

It is common for jazz musicians to skip writing down the transcription. We have found benefits from both written and purely aural approaches. Writing a transcription down allows students to take more time understanding the relationships between the written chords and the notes that are played.

Make It Their Own

Jazz is like a language. When we all learned to talk, we didn't start speaking original sentences right away; we talked like our parents, uncle Phil, an older sister, or an odd cousin from Spokane. All these influences added vocabulary, cadence, style, and ways of thinking to our speech. Over time, those sources coalesced into a unique way of speaking, easily identified as our own. Everyone learns like this, and no one ever says it makes children unoriginal. With enough material, the mind/subconscious assembles the child's own way of speaking. Jazz is no different. Yet there's more to each of us than the sum of our influences; it's not enough to simply parrot.

The goal of transcribing is *not* to end up sounding like someone else. Rather, it is to absorb an artist's way of combining information and to deepen one's understanding of rhythm and style. The more jazz musicians do that, the more ways they learn to organize harmonic language, melodic shape, and compelling rhythm. In short, they are freer to go where they want, unrestricted in their harmonic, rhythmic, and melodic choices. The ultimate goal is complete chromatic and rhythmic freedom; the ability to go where we want, when we want, and how we want, while staying connected to and supporting the other musicians. In other words, we're developing the freedom to make space for every individual voice on the bandstand, including our own.

An individual voice, developed with the intention to connect with other musicians, may be the most prized achievement in jazz. Truthfully, your students *cannot* sound like anyone else. They will, at most, sound like a close second (if that). To keep them from embracing imitation too literally, you, the teacher, should remind them early on that their goal should be to find their own voice. Primarily, students need to imitate in order to hear and feel elements of jazz language such as groove, inflection, phrasing, interaction, harmony, and feeling. When they learn a solo, we want it to inspire their own creative choices. *They should make it their own.* There is good reason for this. It's our view that no jazz musician should copy someone else and present those sounds as their own. Remind your students to have more respect than that for the artists who paid a life to create their sound.

A Few Examples of Creative Practice Inspired by Transcribing

To introduce transcribing as a means to develop your personal vocabulary, here are two lines that might be played by jazz masters such as Sonny Rollins or Charlie Parker, played over a D–G7 progression.

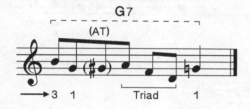

As you can see, you have the tools to understand every melodic device in these lines. Triads and 7th chords are bracketed and labeled with a chord symbol to indicate the structure implied. Approach tones (labeled "AT" and "ATs") are in parentheses.

Beyond practicing structures, we can emulate the shape of a line. The shape of this line is particularly effective: it hovers around the starting point for a bit, rises some, falls back down to the starting point, and then rises quickly to an even higher note:

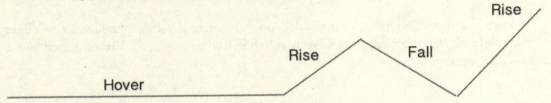

Practice the shape or contour of the line by creating a line that hovers, goes up, falls, and then rises even higher. For example:

In these examples, the shape unfolds for three or four bars; but you could easily stretch that out to eight or even sixteen bars. The importance of interesting shape cannot be overstated.

In the first measure of the example below, the soloist uses the ♭3, 5, ♭7, 9 structure on D– that appears in the first example above. The next measure is labeled G7, but the notes you see don't really correspond to what you normally think of as G7:

The analysis we added tells you the ♭3, 5, ♭7, 9 structure from measure 1 is simply repeated in F minor starting on beat 4 of bar 1. (By now, you likely know what we're about to say: *If you're not early, you're late.*) We call this a parallel phrase.

Playing this example makes it obvious that playing an F minor structure over a G7 sounds very good and resolves to C major easily. You can do this in any key, playing over the V7 by superimposing a Dorian scale built a minor 3rd above the II–7 chord.

It's not necessary, however, to have parallel phrases on D minor and F minor for the line to be effective. Here's a different line for the F minor that works well:

Once again, the sound of F–7 is *anticipated* by a beat. If you hung out with chapter 13, you may recognize the ♯9, ♭9 to 5 which we practiced. In transcribing the following line, you might feel confused about all the accidentals in the line over the written G7:

What you are seeing is nothing more than a common respelling of an altered dominant (see chapter 11). In this case, it's respelled as an A♭– (Δ7). (And, yes, it showed up a beat early. Again. Anticipating. Seriously. Do it.) Significantly, the line moves by half-step from the sound of D–7 to the sound of A♭– (Δ7), ensuring a smooth transition and a strong sense of momentum.

Sometimes, rather than analyzing a progression, it's also useful to analyze what players do with a single chord. Let's take the example of a C major chord lasting two measures:

In the example above you can see that the soloist has played four notes of C major, a D–7 arpeggio, and two more notes of C major. Adding the D–7 arpeggio gives the line more momentum than if it were just C major throughout.

Right away, you can see possibilities. If the soloist, Charlie Parker in this case, can superimpose a D minor seventh, how about a D minor triad? Here are a couple of examples:

Let's take it a step further. If we have a D–7, how about trying a D–7(♭5) (i.e., Dø) instead?

That still works well. How about an F minor triad (the top three notes of Dø)? We'll add a B♭ to replace the D:

This also works. Now, if you want to try something extremely dangerous, let's try inserting a B∆7:

The sky's the limit. Encourage your students to experiment. The only rule is to connect the new material by half-step if possible.

It's our hope that you feel confident with the tools you have for understanding every note in these transcribed melodic lines. If you're not so confident, by all means, contact us. We're always glad to explain a concept you might be having trouble with. With your help, your students' transcriptions can go way beyond imitation: they can inspire creativity.

CHAPTER 17

THE BENEFITS OF PLAY

Why We Teach Jazz

Well, friends and colleagues . . .

Thanks for making it this far with us. For much of this book, we've talked about the *mechanics* of becoming a jazz musician. We have touched on the *spirit* of this music a few times too. And that's where we have decided to end this book: by hanging out on the question, "Why teach jazz?"

No doubt you will, at some point in your career, encounter those who feel pressure to cut costs by doing away with silly things like music programs. We have seen jazz programs be among the first to get cut, as some administrators and parents may believe they don't serve real needs. In response to that, we've put together a list of the benefits we've seen come into our lives, and our students' lives, by learning jazz.

A Word about a Word: *Play*

Before we dive in, we need to make sure we are all on the same page about something: there's a reason we use the word *play* to describe what we do as jazz musicians. The word *play*, as author Christopher Wallis points out, refers to doing something *that has no purpose outside itself*. We feel this is true of music, and perhaps especially true of jazz, an art form rooted in spontaneous creation. Like any art form, the purpose of jazz is *to play* jazz. (In this sense, *play* may as well be a synonym for *live*.) It turns out, play is where humans learn attributes like empathy and compassion.[*] What's more, you can quickly ruin the benefits of play by doing it for any reason other than play itself. *If you structure kids' play time in order to practice empathy, the play will cease to be play.* The conditions will no longer exist for empathy (or any other benefit of play) to bloom. In the same way, the fruits of learning jazz (outlined below) only flourish when our students get to *play for the sake of playing*.

The benefits of playing jazz are just that: benefits, extras, ancillaries. Like all play (and any meaningful human endeavor), the value of jazz (and other musical languages) is intrinsic and even essential. Here in the United States, we live in a country where many have lost sight of this. A great number have stumbled into thinking that something only has value if it is *useful*. We have seen the weight of this reasoning placed on the shoulders of our young people, as many talk in ways that would reduce their personhood to the question of *usefulness*. We feel compelled to ask, "Useful to whom?" This view can harm young people.

---

[*] For an entertaining and informative foray into the subject of play, we highly recommend the podcast *Radiolab* and the episode "The Science of Play."

The question "What's it for?" should never be leveled at a human being or, by extension, an art form.

The Effects of Jazz: Talking Points for Admin and Parents

Still, you may find yourself in a position where you need to advocate for jazz in your music program. In that spirit, we want to offer some language that may help you talk with administrators and parents about the *effects* of this music on people who play it; talking points on how learning jazz improvisation can benefit our students. We've seen manifestations of every one of these in their lives.

- **Adaptability.** Jazz creates space for difference by enhancing—rather than sacrificing—each person's individuality. Because of its emphasis on collective interplay, when we teach jazz, we're preparing our students to be flexible and to work creatively with others. This feels significant to us since our students are inheriting a world in which change will be a defining part of their lives. Jazz improvisation requires one to respond to an ever-changing musical landscape full of unexpected twists and turns, and then to integrate these new realities into a performance.

- **Community.** To play jazz, students must make room for their peers while staying true to their own voices. And, because they must learn to listen to their bandmates' playing with no agenda, they develop empathy and awareness for each other.

- **Confidence.** Because there's no time to second-guess while improvising, students learn to trust themselves. They get more comfortable making decisions and owning them.

- **Connection.** Our culture/society is more divided than at any time within memory. We seek individuality and unity but seem to find little of either that we can hold onto. In a conversation with John McNeil, Zen scholar Alan Watts spoke about jazz as the one area in Western culture where people can immerse themselves in a group without losing their individuality, where both cooperation and individual freedom of expression are equally combined. We have seen our students experience this balance between individuality and community, firsthand.

- **Cognition.** Students who learn jazz are learning skills that reach well beyond music. Playing jazz takes focus, concentration, visualization, and the ability to solve problems quickly. Young people who develop these skills tend to be quicker thinkers. Plus, they become more aware of the need for preparation.

- **Understanding.** Psychologist Boris Cyrulnik writes about the human capacity for resilience in the face of trauma. Based on a lifetime of research, he argues that trauma survivors must find a place to tell their stories—with complete honesty—in a way that is both safe and accepted by their community. As an abstract language, jazz can provide exactly that. Jazz and blues are cultural vessels with freedom and resilience in their DNA, and each listener interprets any message in their own way. They can connect us to a tradition of storytelling too personal to safely say with words.

- **Healing.** In terms of healing social divisions, jazz has tremendous potential. Decades ago, the late night/early morning jam session culture arose from the fact that it was taboo for black and white musicians to play together during regular hours. Right from the start, this creative cooperation threw off artificial divides. If it had the power to do that in the heart of Jim Crow America, we think it just may have the power to do that today. In fact, jazz personally brought author Ryan Nielsen face to face with the biases he inherited growing up, confronted him with their absurdity, and walked him through letting go of those biases without coddling his fears.

- **Freedom through discipline.** Jazz students will practice for hundreds of hours to develop freedom of expression. Far from self-indulgence, the choice to do something (or not) requires practice and practice requires discipline.

Jazz is not the only way to develop these attributes, but we do believe that it is an especially direct way. *Playing* jazz can provide a space for these attributes to develop naturally as our students experience and deal with an ever-changing musical environment. We can hardly think of a more pressing skill set, or a more effective laboratory for our students or ourselves. Out of a system designed to erase personhood, those who created this music affirmed it in the most remarkable of ways.

The greatest compliment a veteran jazz musician can give is, "They're telling the truth." On the flipside, the most concerning critique is, "They sound good, but they're not telling the truth." The young people we have had the pleasure of working with are starving for truth-telling and authenticity. Jazz is about saying the things your students don't feel safe to say elsewhere. Taught the right way, in the right spirit, it can provide an authentic, honest encounter with self and life—one made possible by collaborating with peers.

We wish you the best as you discover this music side by side with your students. And remember, we really are just an email away . . .

John McNeil and Ryan Nielsen
www.mcneiljazz.com
www.ryanstrumpet.com

APPENDIX: JAZZ CHORD SYMBOLS

This appendix will help you understand jazz chord symbols. We have placed examples of possible chord symbols over each scale. Every symbol over a given scale is equivalent: they all mean that one scale. The variety of jazz chord symbols can feel overwhelming at times, and we hope this helps you interpret the symbols you may come across. Whenever a minor respelling is useful (see chapter 11), we have included it next to the appropriate chord/scale.

Some of the chords in this appendix have two scales: a common spelling and a "defining sound." Every note of a defining scale can be used as a point of rest. This is not so with the common spelling. Each time we show two scales, your students can use either the common spelling or the defining scale in their improvisations.

Major Scales and Symbols

Major

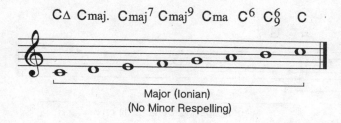

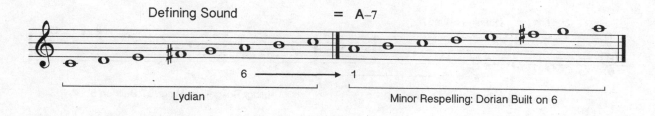

Lydian

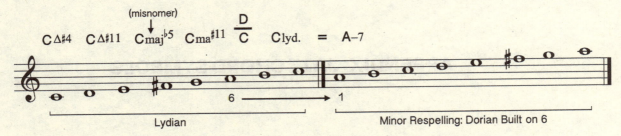

Theoretically, the Cmaj(♭5) is a misnomer, but it's still in common enough use as a symbol for Lydian that you should know about it.

Major (♯5)

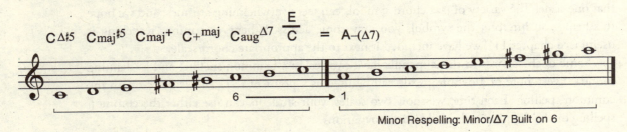

Dominant Scales and Symbols

Dominant (Mixolydian)

Remember: Only the defining sound lets you use every note as a resting point in the line.

APPENDIX: JAZZ CHORD SYMBOLS   147

Dominant Sus

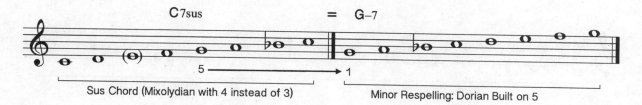

Lydian Dominant

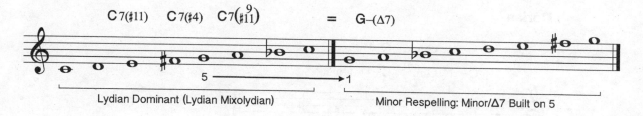

Dominant (♭9 13)

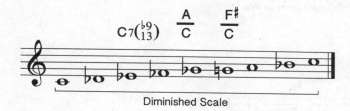

Altered Dominant

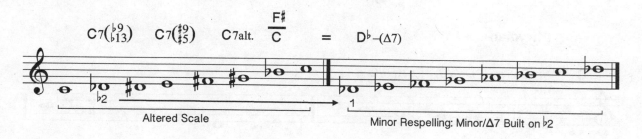

Dominant (♭9)

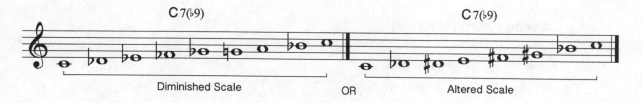

Augmented Dominant

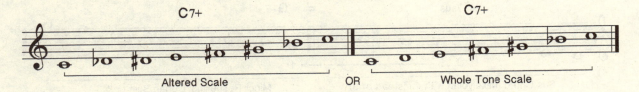

Minor and Diminished Scales and Symbols

Dorian

Reminder: In jazz, Dorian is the default minor scale.

Minor/△7 (Melodic Minor)

Phrygian

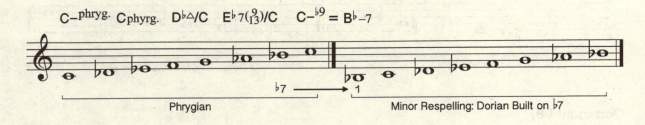

Aeolian (Natural Minor)

Half-Diminished (Locrian and Locrian ♯2)

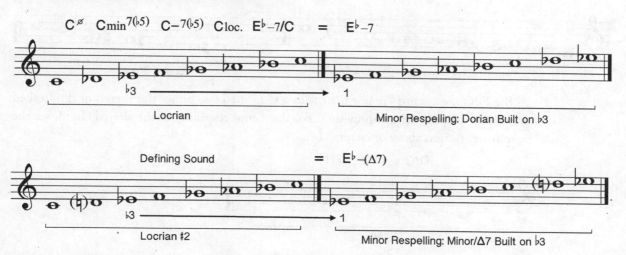

As before, only the defining sound allows your students to use every note as a point of rest in the line.

Diminished

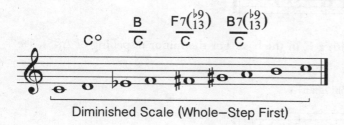

Slash Chords

Slash chords are fairly common in jazz, and can feel puzzling if they are new to you. The slash chord has two parts. The part before (or sometimes above) the slash indicates a chord, usually a triad. The part after (or below) the slash indicates the bass note.

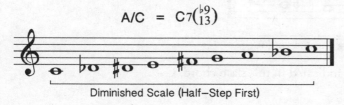

The A/C symbol means an A major triad with a C in the bass. The chord/scale is diminished.

The F♯/C means an F♯ major triad with a C in the bass. Either the altered or diminished scales can be played while improvising. For the minor respelling of the altered chord, see the "Dominant" section above or chapter 11.

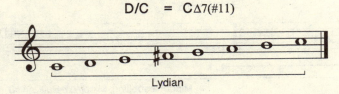

The D/C means a D major triad with a C in the bass. For the minor respelling of Lydian, see the "Major" section above or chapter 11.

E/C means an E major triad with a C in the bass. For the minor respelling of Δ(♯5), see the "Major" section above.

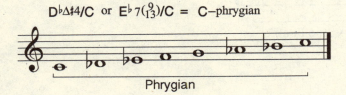

For the minor respelling of Phrygian, see the "Minor" section above.

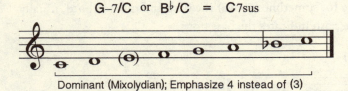

The minor respelling is already indicated in this slash chord: G–7.

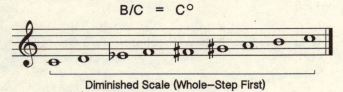

The B/C means a B major triad with a C♮ in the bass. Note that this diminished scale begins with a whole-step.

INDEX

For the benefit of digital users, indexed terms that span two pages (e.g., 52–53) may, on occasion, appear on only one of those pages.

7th-chord shapes, 59

advocacy, 142–43
Aebersold, Jamey, 32
aeolian. *See* chord symbols
Allen, Geri, 132
anticipation, 37–38, 61, 98–99, 108, 111
approach tones
  7th chords and, 59–60
    on major, 59
    on minor, 59
  II–7|V7|IΔ7 and, 110–12
  four-and-five-note, 60–61
    on major, 61
    on minor, 61
  half-step below, 35–37
    on major triads, 38
    on piano and guitar voicings, 38–39
  scale-step above, 41–43
  second scale degree as, 25–27
  three-note
    below/above/below, 53–55
    chromatic, 55–57
    on major, 57
    on minor, 56
  two-note
    above/below, 47–49
    chromatic, 49–51
    on major, 51
    on minor, 51
Armstrong, Louis, 133

backgrounds
  how to create, 12, 99
  melodic, 79–80
Baker, Chet, 74, 110
barline
  Moving the, 107–9
Basie, Count, 133
bass
  bass lines using diatonic thirds, 68
  bass lines using triad pitches, 21–22
  ornamenting lines with approach tones, 46
  ornamenting lines with second scale degree, 34
  respelling chords and, 89
  role while adding and dropping beats, 108

beats
  adding and dropping on II–7|V7|IΔ7, 110–12
  adding and dropping on dominant cycle, 107–9
Blakey, Art, 3, 9, 12
Blues
  1-2-3-5 and, 120–23
  depth of, 5, 113
  encoded derision and, 114
  freedom and, 114
  harmonic form of, 115–20
  harmonic options, 123
  heads, 129–31
  historical context of, 113–15
  jazz musicians spend a lifetime studying, 113
  learning by heart, 125
  melodies, 122
  not sad music, 114
  recommended readings in, 115
  respelling and, 118, 120, 122
  tunes to learn by ear, 125, 127–28, 132–33
    Copacetic, 130
    Listen Here, 131
    Stop Bothering Me, 129
  why we don't begin with, 5–6, 113
Brackeen, Joanne, 132
Brown, Clifford, 3, 132
Brown, Ray, 133

call and response, 4, 9, 35, 53, 93
Caruso, Carmine, xi, 15
change
  adapting to, 142
changes. *See* chords
choice, 1, 2, 11–12, 30
  with triad shapes, 11–12, 13
chords
  changing from chord to chord, 15, 31–32, 72–76, 121
    II–7 to V7, 94–96
    V7 to IΔ7, 93–94, 96–97
    II–7|V7|IΔ7, 93–94, 98–99, 102–3, 110–12
    dominant cycles, 107–9
    piano and guitar voicings, 100
  choosing sequence for curriculum, 16, 96, 97, 110
  common tones between, 32, 73–74, 100
  memorizing, 118

chord-scales, 7
    diatonic 4ths and, 81
    diatonic 7th chords and, 81
    diatonic thirds and, 63–66
    diatonic triads and, 77–79
chord symbols
    aeolian, 8
    altered dominant, 88
    dominant, 9, 88
    extensions, 8
    half-diminished, 89
    how to read, 7–9, 83
    lydian, 89
    major, 8
    melodic minor, 83
        respelling and, 85
    minor, 8
        dorian, 7, 25, 73
            as default minor, 6, 8, 89
            respelling and, 85
    mixolydian (*see* chord symbols: dominant)
    quality, 7, 8
    respelling chords, 83–86
        altered dominant and, 88
        dominant and, 88
        examples in tunes, 85–86
        half-diminished and, 89
        lydian and, 89
        not for rhythm section, 85, 89
        parallel structures and, 87
        theory behind, 88–89
    roots, 7–8
    superlocrian (*see* chord symbols: altered dominant)
    three parts of, 7, 9
    why so confusing in jazz, 83
Clark, Sonny, 133
cognition, 142
Coltrane, John, 3, 77, 132, 133
combining materials, 81
common Tones, 32
comping, 19
cooperation, 142
Corea, Chick, 3
Cyrulnik, Boris, 142

Davis, Miles, 3, 49, 53, 55, 105, 132, 133
    designing melody between 3 and 9, 105
dominant. *See* chord symbols
dominant ♭9, 110–12
dominant cycles
    1-2-3-5 and, 103–5
    3-5-7-9 arpeggios and, 105–7
dorian. *See* chord symbols
drummers
    artists for listening, 22
    gumption to encounter, 22
drums
    basic technique and kicks, 22–24
    independence and, 23, 38
    feathering the bass drum, 23
    hi-hat, 24
    orchestrating with sections, 38
    power to destroy, 22
    priorities for, 24
    ride cymbal, 22, 38
    upbeats and, 38

economy, 16
Ellington, Duke, 114, 132, 133
email
    authors', 6, 143
empathy, 142
Evans, Bill, 3

Farmer, Art, 93
fear of failure as barrier, 14
Foster, Al, 38
freedom
    Discipline and, 143
Freeman, Russ, 110
fun, 11–12

Gillespie, Dizzy, 94, 96, 105, 114, 115
Gillespie, Luke, 19
Gordon, Dexter, 58
guitar
    basic voicings, 20–21, 69
    comping and, 19, 69
    voicing altered dominant, 90
    voicing half-diminished, 91
    voice leading and, 100

Hancock, Herbie, 133
Harris, Gene, 133
healing, 142–43
Henderson, Joe, 3, 132
Hubbard, Freddie, 3, 132

Ignatius Kendell. *See* Kendell, Ignatius
improvise
    everyone can, 1
individuality, 142
    unity in, 142

jam session culture, 142–43
jargon
    avoid, 4
jazz
    universal roots of, 115
Johnson, Jay Jay, 102
Jones, Elvin, 3

Kendell, Ignatius, 50

Levine, Mark, 19
lines
    developing longer, 27–30, 43–45, 56–57, 68, 71–72, 99–100
    strength of descending, 65, 67, 68, 79–80
listening, 19
    recommended albums, 3–4
    recommended blues heads, 127–31, 132–33
    recommended tunes
        Alright, Okay, You Win, 125

An Oscar for Treadwell, 96
Bag's Groove, 127
Bloomdido, 94
Blowin' the Blues Away, 25
Blueport, 93
Blues for Duane, 127
Bouncing with Bud, 98
Chi Chi, 107
Confirmation, 101
Everyday I Have the Blues, 125
Get Happy, 102
Happy Little Sunbeam, 110
If I Were a Bell, 55
It's You or No One, 58
Love for Sale, 49
Moment's Notice, 77
My Groove, Your Move, 41
Oleo, 53
One by One, 9
On the Ginza, 12
Pent-Up House, 63
Roll Call, 43
Saint Thomas, 35
Shaw 'Nuff, 105
Sister Sadie, 27
Sonnymoon for Two, 71
Soul Shoutin', 79
Speak No Evil, 47
Splanky, 128
This I Dig of You, 72
Work, 127
Liston, Melba, 132
Longley, Michael, 113
Lydian. *See* chord symbols

McLean, Jackie, 132
melodic minor. *See* Chord symbols
metronome
   in rehearsal, 5, 32, 105
   on beats 2 and 4, 5
Mingus, Charles, 132
mistakes
   learning to ignore, 105, 107
mixolydian. *See* chord symbols
Mobley, Hank, 41, 43, 72, 132
modes. *See* chord-scales
Monk, Thelonious, 132, 133
Mulligan, Gerry, 93

natural minor. *See* aeolian
non-judgmental, 11–12

organization without predictability, 65, 71, 105, 109
ornaments. *See* approach tones

Parker, Charlie, 94, 96, 101, 105, 107, 133
Peterson, Oscar, 3, 133
piano
   basic voicings, 18–19, 69
   blues and, 133
   comping and, 19, 69, 124
      diatonic thirds and, 69

   ornamenting voicings with approach tones, 38–39, 46
   voicing altered dominant, 90
   voicing half-diminished, 91
   voicing the minor iiø V7alt, 91
   voice leading and, 100
Pilafian, Sam. xi
play, 141–42
   empathy and, 141
Powell, Bud, 98, 133
practice
   how jazz artists practice, 6
pressure
   permission not to feel any, 4
problem solving, 142

range
   adjusting for student needs, 16
recordings
   play-along, 32, 108
respelling chords, 83–84
   how to, 84–85
rhythm
   and-of-four as downbeat, 37, 61, 98–99
   basic jazz rhythms, 13, 27
   designing and critiquing, 16–17, 45
   hemiolas in jazz, 32–34, 71, 72
   in practice, 5
   implementing with triads, 12–16
   more advanced, 32–34
   stream of 8th-notes note compelling, 72
   syncopation, 36–37, 42, 45

shythm section. *See also individual instruments*
   bass, 21–22, 34, 46, 68, 89
   drums, 22–24, 38
   general tips for, 17
   guitar, 20–21, 39, 90, 100
   piano, 18–19, 38–39, 46, 69, 90, 91, 100, 124, 133
   what to do during triad practice, 12

Roach, Max, 3
Rollins, Sonny, 3, 35, 63, 71, 105, 133
root triad, 9–12
   as tonal center of gravity, 16, 63
   why start with, 16
rote memory, 2

scale drills, 4, 9–10, 12, 25, 28, 41, 43–44, 47–48, 49–50, 53–54, 55–56, 58
   7th chords and, 58
   thirds and, 28, 41, 43–44, 47–48, 49–50, 53–54, 55–56, 58
   triads and, 78
scales
   diatonic 4ths and, 81
   diatonic 7th chords and, 81
   diatonic thirds and, 63–66
   diatonic triads and, 77–79
   don't begin by improvising with, 6
Scott, Shirley, 3, 79, 133
Shaw, Woody, 133

Shorter, Wayne, 47
Silver, Horace, 3–4, 25, 27, 133
simplifying, 14
    Carmine Caruso and, 15
    tasks that feel complex, 14
    three-note approaches, 61–62
singing, 9–10, 11, 26, 35, 48, 53, 63, 64, 74, 93
    backgrounds and, 99
    Chet Baker and, 74
    tetrachords and, 66–67
storytelling, 142
Strayhorn, Billy, 114
structures
    melodic, 6, 101
students
    how we know they're creative, 103
subconscious, 1–2
superlocrian. *See* chord symbols
swing
    and-of-four as downbeat, 37, 61, 98–99
    Eighth notes, 14
    Syncopation and, 36–37, 42, 45

talking points. *See* advocacy
telling the truth, 143
Terry, Clark. v–vi, 3, 133
    impact in New York studio scene, v
tetrachords, 66–67
transcribing, 135
    creative practice and, 137–40
    how to, 135–36
    originality and, 135
    purpose of, 136–37
trauma, 142
triads
    diatonic, 77–79
triad shapes, 11–12, 13
tunes to begin with, 32
turnaround, 123

understanding, 142
unpredictable. *See* Organization without predictability
useful
    dangers of, 141–42

visualizing, 10, 12, 142
    motor skills and, 105
    pushing it into the future, 105, 106–7
voice leading
    7 to 3, 93–94, 101–3
    dominant cycles and, 104–5, 107–9
    from II–7 to V7, 94–96
    from V7 to IΔ7, 96–97, 101–2
    on the II–7|V7|IΔ7, 93–94, 98–99, 110–12

Watts, Alan, 142
Williams, Mary Lou, 133

Young, Larry, 4